Sharks, the Super Fish

Sharks were well established long before dinosaurs evolved. They survived the changes that millions of years ago caused the extinction of dinosaurs and other creatures, and continue to thrive in the oceans of modern times.

SHARKS,
the Super Fish

BY HELEN RONEY SATTLER

ILLUSTRATED BY JEAN DAY ZALLINGER

LOTHROP, LEE & SHEPARD BOOKS · NEW YORK

ACKNOWLEDGMENTS

I would like to express my deepest appreciation and thanks to Dr. Eugenie Clark, Professor of Ichthyology at the University of Maryland, for reading the completed manuscript and checking the drawings for accuracy. Her comments and suggestions were invaluable. I also extend thanks to Dr. Donald Nelson of the University of California at Long Beach for sharing his valuable time with me to discuss sharks, and for giving me copies of his reports to read.

In addition to the references listed in "For Further Reading," I am grateful to the following authors for information gleaned from their papers published in scientific journals and books: John Bass, M. V. L. Bennet, Joel Cohen, Chuck Davis, Perry Gilbert, R. Curtis Graeber, John H. Harding, Phillip C. Heemstra, Edward S. Hodgson, Joseph John, Richard H. Johnson, Yasuji Katsuki and staff, George Llano, John E. McCosker, Harold McCormick and staff, Frederick H. Martini, Peter Matthiessen, Robert F. Mathewson, Arthur A. Myrberg, Jr., R. Glenn Northcutt, A. K. O'Gower, Tom Philbin, John E. Randall, B. L. Roberts, Pat Smith, Carsten Stroud, Jeremiah S. Sullivan, Ron and Valerie Taylor, Mark Wexler, and Bernard Zahuranec. I also thank Ruth Bartles for suggesting this book.

LIBRARY OF CONGRESS CATALOGING IN PUBLICATION DATA

Sattler, Helen Roney.
Sharks, the super fish.
Bibliography: p.
Summary: Discusses sharks and their behavior and includes tips for swimmers and a lengthy dictionary of shark types, describing each one.
I. Sharks—Juvenile literature. [1. Sharks] I. Zallinger, Jean, ill. II. Title.
QL638.9.S26   1986   597′.31   84-4381
ISBN 0-688-03993-6

Dedicated
in memory of
my brother Charles and
his wife Irma

Contents

bull sharks *(C. leucas)*

Chapter 1

Rulers of the Sea

S UPER FISH patrol the oceans of the world. They have been patrolling them for millions of years. These fish are called sharks. Just as humans rule the land, sharks are masters of the seas. They may be the most feared and hated animals on earth.

This is sad, because there are many more things to admire about sharks than to fear. No other creature is so well suited to rule the sea. They are among the oldest, the smartest, and the most beautiful of all fish. Some are the largest fish, and a few are the most dangerous.

People are afraid of sharks because they hear only about those that have attacked or killed humans. These sharks deserve to be treated with extreme caution, but most sharks are not dangerous.

There are more than three hundred kinds of sharks. Only thirty of these types have ever attacked humans. Most sharks are shy and flee from people. As a matter of fact, far more people have died from bee stings than shark attacks. Still, there are many more people who are afraid of sharks than there are people who are afraid of bees.

All sharks should not be judged by the actions of a few. When you hear the word dog, do you picture an animal bred and trained to be a vicious guard dog or a friendly house pet? Or do you think of an animal as big as a Great Dane or as small as a Chihuahua? Like dogs, each type of shark is different. Some are dangerous, some are friendly.

Most sharks have bodies that are shaped like missiles, but some are

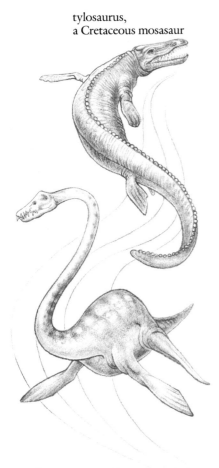

tylosaurus,
a Cretaceous mosasaur

elasmosaurus, a Cretaceous plesiosaur

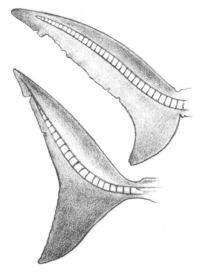

shark tails

flat and others are long like a snake. Although most sharks are smaller than a man, some are bigger than a moving van. There is one that is smaller than a child's hand.

Sharks are strong, healthy creatures with few enemies. No living thing can take better care of itself than a shark. They are very cautious animals.

They have been taking care of themselves for more than 300 million years. There were sharks before there were dinosaurs. Some that looked very much like those living today swam with mosasaurs (MO-sah-sawrs) and plesiosaurs (PLEE-see-o-sawrs). Mosasaurs, plesiosaurs, and dinosaurs died out, but sharks didn't. When changes took place on earth, sharks changed, and survived. They found new ways to meet their needs.

They grew thick, tough skin to protect themselves from enemies. Instead of scales like other fish, their skin is covered with tiny sharp teeth called dermal denticles (DER-mal DEN-ti-cles) or "skin teeth." In most sharks, these teeth are set very close together and feel like sandpaper. They are sharp enough to take the skin off your hand and hard enough to dull a knife.

Sharks developed color patterns on their skins which make them difficult to capture. They blend so well into their watery world that they are hard to see. Most sharks are dull gray or brown. All except deep sea species have lighter undersides and darker tops. To an enemy swimming above, they look like the dark water around them. From below, they look like sunlight shining on the water. Some have patterns on their backs that blend with the bottom of the ocean.

The skeleton of a shark has changed very little through the ages. A shark's backbone is made of a soft material called cartilage (KART-il-lej). Cartilage is the stuff your ears and the tip of your nose are made of. Sharks don't have ribs. Muscles fastened to the skin and backbone help hold the body in shape. The pressure of the water helps too. When a shark swims fast, its body gets quite hard. Sometimes when a shark is taken out of water, its insides pull apart, and it dies.

The backbones of bony fish stop at their tails, and the upper and lower parts of the tail-fin are usually equal in length. In almost all sharks, the upper tail lobe is longer than the lower, and the backbone goes to the tip of the upper lobe of the tail. This makes the tail strong. The shark uses its tail to move itself through water.

In the water, a shark is one of the most graceful of all creatures. Because of its streamlined body and soft skeleton, it needs very little energy to move. They are perfectly designed for life in the sea.

Sharks do not swim like other fish. They glide more like airplanes. Simple sweeps of the tail and snakelike movements of the body propel them through the water. The long side or pectoral (PEK-tor-al) fins are like the wings of an airplane. They help the shark to go up or down; they are not flapped or moved back and forth. The tall back or dorsal (DOR-sal) fins and the pelvic fins, like the tail of an airplane, keep the shark from rolling. A shark cannot stop suddenly or swim backward. It changes direction by bending its limber body in a sharp curve.

Airplanes are heavier than air, and a shark's body is heavier than sea water. If a shark stops moving, it sinks to the bottom. Therefore, if it wants to keep afloat, it must never stop swimming.

Bony fish have sacs of gas called swim bladders inside their bodies to keep them afloat. Sharks do not have swim bladders. Some gulp air at the surface and hold it in their stomachs. This helps them stay afloat for a while. Many sharks have large amounts of oil in their livers. Oil is lighter than water; therefore, the oil makes sharks lighter and enables them to swim slower without sinking.

When patrolling, sharks swim only three to five miles in an hour, just enough to keep from sinking. But when they are chasing food or escaping enemies, some can swim very fast—up to forty miles per hour. Few fish can swim faster.

Also, most sharks must keep moving so they can breathe easily. All fish breathe by taking oxygen from water with their gills. Bony fish have one gill opening on each side of their bodies. They pump water over their gills. Sharks have five, six, or seven gill openings on each side. Some can pump water over their gills if they are caught on a hook or resting on the bottom. But usually most sharks make water flow over their gills by swimming with their mouths open. This forces water to flow into their mouths and out through their gill slits. This means they must swim constantly, but it takes less energy for a streamlined shark to swim day and night without stopping than it would to pump water all the time.

Some sharks spend long periods lying on the sea floor. Others rest in special caves. The water in these caves has more oxygen in it than the

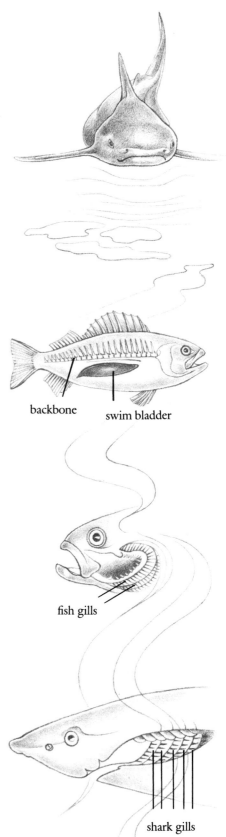

backbone   swim bladder

fish gills

shark gills

nurse shark (*C. cirratum*)

water outside. When in these caves, a shark does not need to work hard to get oxygen.

Sometimes a shark stays in the cave for several hours. It looks as though it is asleep, but it is not. A shark may rest, but it does not sleep, at least not the way humans do. When it leaves the cave, it is ready to look for food.

zebra shark *(S. varium)*

Chapter 2

Super Hunters

SHARKS are among the best hunters in the world. Even day-old pups go looking for food. These super hunters seem to be born hungry.

Many people think that sharks will eat anything at any time. That is not true. Sharks are carnivores, which means they eat flesh, but they eat only what they need. Most hunt at dawn or at dusk, many feed at night, but a few feed during the day. A shark's hunger can be satisfied with one good meal. This meal sometimes lasts a long time because the shark needs so little energy to swim. Some sharks are able to hold food in their stomachs without digesting it. If allowed to eat their fill, they can go three or more months between meals.

Like wolves, sharks prefer food that is easily caught. They eat dead animals when they can find them. But their normal diet is living animals that have been weakened or injured. Usually these are smaller than themselves. However, if they are very hungry, sharks may attack larger animals.

Most sharks eat fish which are swallowed whole. But there are very few creatures in the ocean that at least one shark won't eat. Stingrays are a favorite food of hammerhead sharks. Great white sharks eat smaller sharks and seals and whales. Smoothhound sharks eat only clams and other shellfish. And the largest sharks—whale and basking sharks—eat plankton, which are tiny shrimplike sea animals.

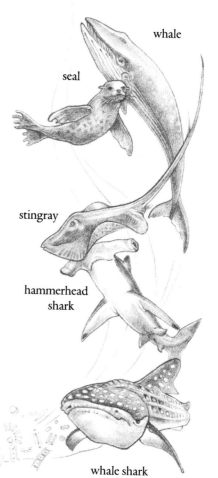

whale

seal

stingray

hammerhead
shark

whale shark

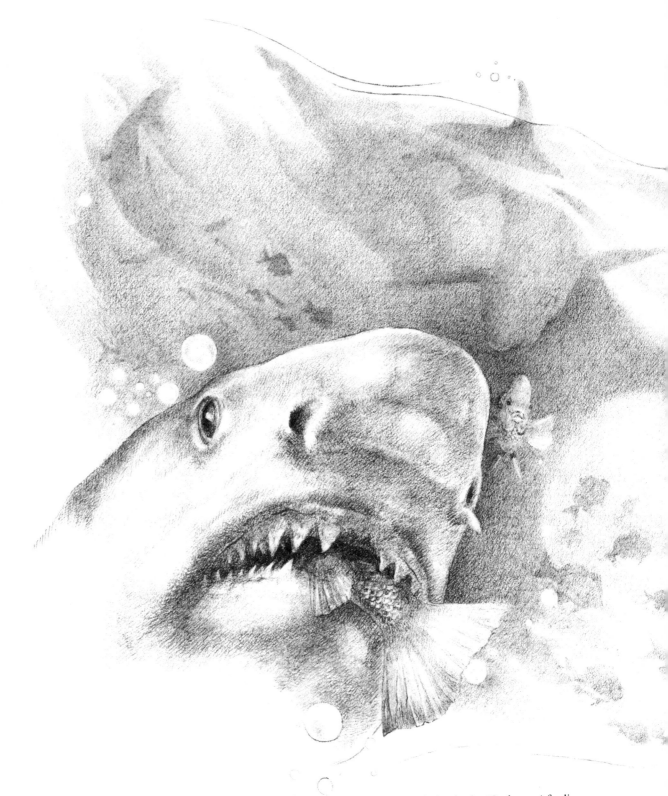

dusky sharks *(C. obscurus)* feeding

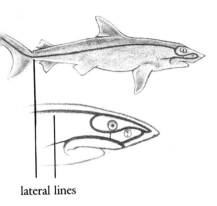

lateral lines

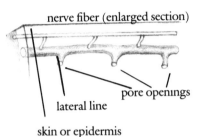

nerve fiber (enlarged section)

pore openings

lateral line

skin or epidermis

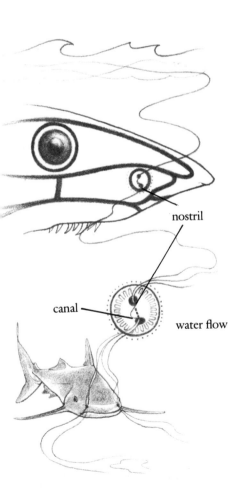

nostril

canal

water flow

Sharks normally don't eat human flesh. Most sharks seem not to like the taste of humans. The majority that bite people release them without tearing off a piece of flesh.

Sharks make no sounds as they travel through the water, but they are good listeners. They have very sensitive ears. You cannot see the ears because sharks have only inner ears, which are located under the skin, just behind the eyes.

As sharks patrol the sea they are alert to signals that tell them an easy meal is nearby. Often the first signal they receive is the low pulsing sounds made by the struggles of a wounded fish, the splashings of swimming mammals, or the flutterings of feeding fish or schools of fish. These sounds are too low for a human ear to hear, but sharks can hear them a thousand yards away.

In addition to their ears, sharks have special fluid-filled organs called lateral lines (LAT-er-al lines). These are located just under the skin on the sharks' snouts and along both sides of their bodies. They help sharks to sense or "feel" the tiniest motions made by any object in the water.

Sharks also have a very good sense of smell, just as good as their hearing, but odors take longer to reach them than sounds. They can pick up scents only by swimming upstream in the strongest ocean currents. In a good current they can smell one drop of blood in several million drops of water. They can follow the scent of a wounded or frightened fish from a mile away.

Sharks' nostrils are set wide apart on the underside of their snouts. They locate prey by following the nostril that receives the strongest odor, zigzagging along the trail to home in on the scent.

When they get within a hundred feet of their prey, sharks use their eyes to zero in on it. It was once thought that sharks did not have good eyesight. We now know that they can see very well. They can see much better in the dark or in murky water than humans can. Tests prove that sharks can also see colors, and they are especially attracted to brightly colored or shiny objects.

Some sharks have tiny eyes, but those that live in deep water have very large eyes. Large eyes help them see better in the dark.

Many sharks have special hard·eyelids called nictitating (NIK-tuh-tate-ing) membranes, which they close during an attack. This protects their eyes from being injured by creatures like octopuses or swordfish. Other sharks protect their eyes by rolling them upward and back.

When their eyes are closed or rolled back, sharks cannot see. Then they use another way to find their food. Tiny pores on the bottoms of their snouts lead to jelly-filled sacs called ampullae of Lorenzini (am-PUL-lee of lor-en-ZEE-nee), which can detect very, very weak electrical fields.

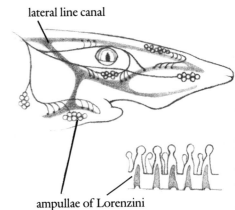

lateral line canal

All living creatures are surrounded by weak electrical fields. A struggling or frightened fish creates a strong electrical current. This current flows through the water. Although it gets weaker as it travels away from the fish, sharks can pick it up. Their ampullae of Lorenzini are the strongest electrical sensors known in nature. A dogfish shark can detect an electrical field that is less than that produced by current passing through a wire which connects two tiny penlight batteries placed a thousand miles apart.

ampullae of Lorenzini

This special sense is used in the last seconds of attack, or when hunting at night. Sharks that feed on the bottom of the ocean use it to locate stingrays or flounders buried under sand.

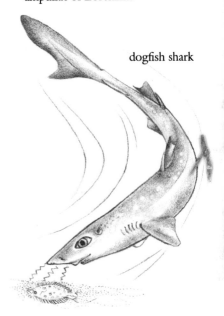

dogfish shark

Many sharks investigate food carefully before attacking it. They circle the animal slowly. Gradually the circle gets smaller until finally they bump the prey with their snouts. If it feels like food, they may take a small bite, which makes the victim bleed. If they like the taste, they eat the prey.

Sometimes the blood brings other sharks. But, more often, it is the vibrations of the feeding shark that brings other sharks. If there are a great many, they may go into a feeding frenzy as each rushes in to get a bite. In their excitement they snap at anything that moves, occasionally even each other.

The jaws of a shark resemble a huge bear trap lined with hundreds of teeth, which are razor sharp and as hard as steel. They are the most powerful jaws on earth. Those of a great white shark can bend a boat's propeller, or even make a hole in the boat. In most sharks, the mouth is located on the underside of the long snout. To bite, a shark thrusts out its lower jaw, draws back its snout, and snaps up its teeth. Contrary to what many people think, a shark does not have to roll over to bite.

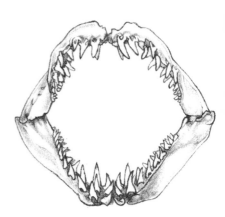

A shark's teeth fall out easily because they are not set in bone. Most sharks lose teeth every time they take a hard bite. But this is no problem. Sharks have four or five rows of spare teeth, each waiting to replace one

jaws of mako shark

band of teeth in upper jaw of whale shark

upper   lower

teeth of silky shark

upper   lower

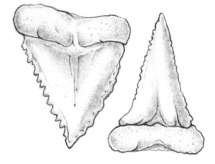

teeth of white shark

upper   lower

teeth of basking shark

upper   lower

teeth of whale shark

that falls out. When not in use, the spare teeth lie flat in the gums. In a lifetime a shark may use up many thousands of teeth. Some get a whole new set every four or five weeks.

No two kinds of sharks have exactly the same kind or size of teeth. In some sharks the upper teeth are thin triangular-shaped knives with sharp points and saw-toothed edges. The lower teeth are often spikelike. When a shark bites, it first sinks the needle-sharp spikes into the prey to hold it, then cuts into the flesh with the knifelike uppers. With a violent shake of its head, the shark removes a huge bite and swallows it whole.

The great white shark's 2.5-inch teeth are the largest. Those of the whale and basking sharks are the smallest. They are no bigger than a baby's fingernail and are not used for catching food. These sharks strain plankton from water with long gill rakers. Those of basking sharks look like giant eyelashes.

A few sharks have teeth that are smooth and flattened like paving stones, which are used to crush clams and snails. Sand tigers and makos have spikelike teeth in both upper and lower jaws. These sharks swallow a whole fish in one gulp. A fifteen-foot tiger shark was once found with two six-foot sharks in its stomach.

Sometimes sharks swallow things they cannot digest. Tiger sharks have been found with many strange things in their stomachs. One had a roll of tar paper, a keg of nails, and a carpenter's square in its stomach. Some people think sharks that swallow such things may have too much oil in their livers. They may be too light to dive or swim properly. Perhaps they need to take on ballast like submarines do. They could get rid of the junk if they wanted to, because most sharks can reject any food they do not like by turning their stomachs inside out.

No animal can hunt or capture food better than a shark. These super hunters have had millions of years to learn about their environment and to adjust to it. And they have the best hunting tools on earth.

upper   lower

teeth of tiger shark

upper   lower

teeth of sand shark

upper   lower

teeth of thresher shark

Chapter 3

Smart Fish

ONCE DURING A STORM, a half-grown whale shark swam into the lagoon of a small Pacific island. It came in on a high tide. When the storm was over, the twenty-six-foot shark was trapped. It couldn't find its way out.

Although sharks are one of the most common creatures in the ocean, we know very little about them. Large sharks are difficult to study because they are hard to find and hard to keep up with. The trapped whale shark gave scientists an opportunity to observe this rare shark.

The scientists became very fond of the young shark and named her Mini. However, they were afraid that she would starve in the small lagoon, so they threw frozen shrimp into the water whenever she passed under their boat. After the third handful, the shark came to the surface and opened her huge jaws. A handful of shrimp was thrown into her mouth. The shark spit them out. But the next day she swallowed some of the shrimp. After that, the shark came to the boat every day to be fed. She would gently bump the boat with her snout to let the scientists know she was there, then she would surface and open her mouth.

One day during a high tide, Mini escaped. Two months later the scientists found her near the island. She bumped the boat with her nose just as she had done in the lagoon. They were surprised. Imagine a shark acting like a well-trained pet! Moreover, she remembered them!

Not very long ago people thought sharks were stupid eating ma-

whale shark

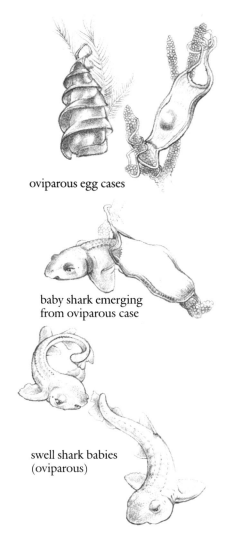

oviparous egg cases

baby shark emerging
from oviparous case

swell shark babies
(oviparous)

baby tiger shark during
development inside its
mother (ovoviviparous)

yolksac

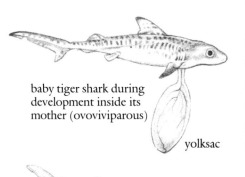

baby blue sharks

chines that couldn't learn anything. Then scientists learned how to keep some sharks alive in pens and tanks so they could study and test them. The scientists discovered that sharks are much smarter than they once imagined. In fact, they have quite large brains and are among the smartest of the fish.

Some sharks have very good attention spans and, as Mini also proved, good memories. Some have been taught to come for food when they hear a buzzer. Others have learned to push a target with their noses and ring a bell for a reward. They have also learned to tell one shape from another and to tell the difference between two colors or patterns. Sharks can easily detect stripes and can distinguish horizontal stripes from vertical stripes.

Sharks can be found almost anywhere in the ocean. Most prefer warm tropical waters, but a few live in icy arctic waters. Some live in the very deepest water of the ocean. Others live in the shallowest water near the shore. A few even live in fresh water lakes and rivers.

Many of the sharks found near the shore are young. Shallow waters are good places for young sharks to grow up, because many small fish and other shark food live there. And usually there are not many large sharks around that might eat the babies.

Baby sharks are called pups. Unlike bony fish, which all hatch from eggs laid in water, shark pups are born in different ways. Some hatch from egg cases laid in water. These odd-shaped horny eggs take eight to fourteen months to hatch. Long threads or tendrils fasten them to branches of coral or seaweed until they hatch.

However, most pups are born alive. Some of these hatch from eggs inside the mother's body and remain there until they are big enough to take care of themselves. This sometimes takes a long time. Spiny dogfish are two years old before they leave their mothers' bodies. Tiger sharks are born in nine months. Other sharks, like hammerheads, blue sharks, and basking sharks, develop inside their mothers without shells; however, they do not suckle after birth as young mammals do.

Mother sharks usually give birth to their pups in the same place year after year. Mothers do not eat while they are in the "nursery." And male sharks never go near it. They might eat one of their own babies by mistake.

Some sharks give birth to only two pups every other year. Some have as many as a hundred at a time, but most have between ten and twenty.

The largest shark egg ever found was twelve inches long. It had a fourteen-inch baby whale shark in it. Newly hatched swell shark pups are only four inches long. Tiger shark pups, which are born alive, are about thirty inches long. Great whites are four feet long.

Newborn pups look almost exactly like their parents. They have teeth and are able to take care of themselves as soon as they are born. Scientists say that baby sharks learn faster than adults. Young sharks are curious and become excited easily. They are more aggressive than adults and should not be teased.

If a shark isn't caught or eaten, it may live to be thirty years old. Some, like sandbar sharks, do not mature until they are twelve years old. Others mature sooner. Some pups are born in the spring or early summer. When the water cools in late fall, they move to warmer waters.

By tagging wild sharks, scientists have learned that many adult sharks travel great distances, migrating north in the spring and returning south again in the fall. A tagged blue shark once traveled 2,700 miles in four months. Others simply go deeper to reach warmer water. On the other hand, some, like nurse or tiger sharks, seldom travel anywhere.

Young sharks usually don't swim with adults. And males seldom swim with females, except during mating season. Some shark species travel in schools, at least during certain times of the year. Some species always travel in packs like wolves. Other sharks travel alone.

Many sharks return to the same area year after year. They pick up the earth's magnetic fields with their ampullae of Lorenzini. Scientists think that sharks may use these ampullae as built-in electro-magnetic compasses to find their way around the ocean. They may use sound or special markings to stay together in schools and to locate mates or enemies.

Sometimes a large shark, like a whitetip, will claim a small portion of a reef. It may allow smaller sharks to swim in its neighborhood, but they must eat a different kind of food, or eat only scraps that the "king of the hill" leaves. They may be struck in the side, if they try to eat some of the king's food. Sometimes another shark moves in and takes over.

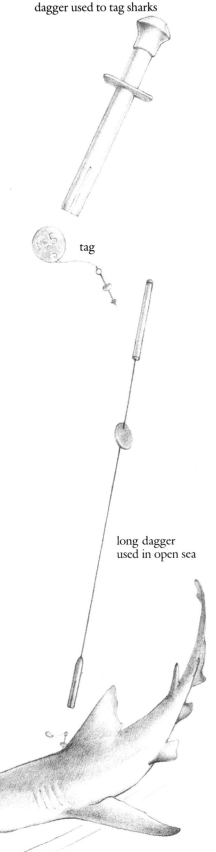

dagger used to tag sharks

tag

long dagger used in open sea

Usually large sharks boss smaller ones, but most give in to hammer-heads—even if they are the same size.

Scientists have learned many things about sharks, but the average person still knows less about them than almost any other creature on earth. One reason we know so little is that although sharks fear few creatures in the ocean, most are shy of humans. They stay away from places where there are many humans—just as coyotes usually stay away from cities. The more scientists learn about these fascinating fish, the more they realize how mistaken people have been about them.

hammerhead shark

Chapter 4

Friends and Foes

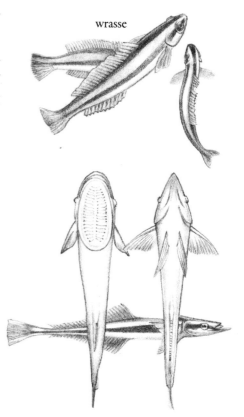

wrasse

SHARKS have few friends. Most creatures flee from them or ignore them. But tiny wrasse and pilot fish are not afraid of sharks. Pilot fish eat scraps left by sharks and swim in their slipstream within inches of the shark's jaws. No one knows exactly why sharks don't eat them. They may be too fast for a shark to catch. Or pilot fish, like wrasse, may eat the tiny crablike creatures that dig into a shark's skin.

Remoras (REM-o-rahs) are not afraid of sharks, either. Remoras are hitchhikers and most sharks have one or two of these little fish as passengers. They fasten themselves to the shark's body with strong suction cups on their heads. The shark doesn't mind because remoras are good housekeepers. They eat many of the crablike pests that live on the shark's body.

Some sharks get rid of these pests by swimming into fresh water at the mouths of rivers. The pests drop off because they don't like fresh water. Then the remoras have a feast. Other sharks go into underwater caves where the water is less salty than the ocean. While there, the crablike creatures loosen their hold, and the remoras vacuum the shark's body clean. When the sharks leave the cave, they are free of the parasites.

Sharks also have few enemies, but there are some creatures that sharks stay away from. Scorpion fish, sea whips, flatfish, and sea cucumbers are poisonous, and sharks do not eat them. Most sharks don't eat porcupine

pilot fish

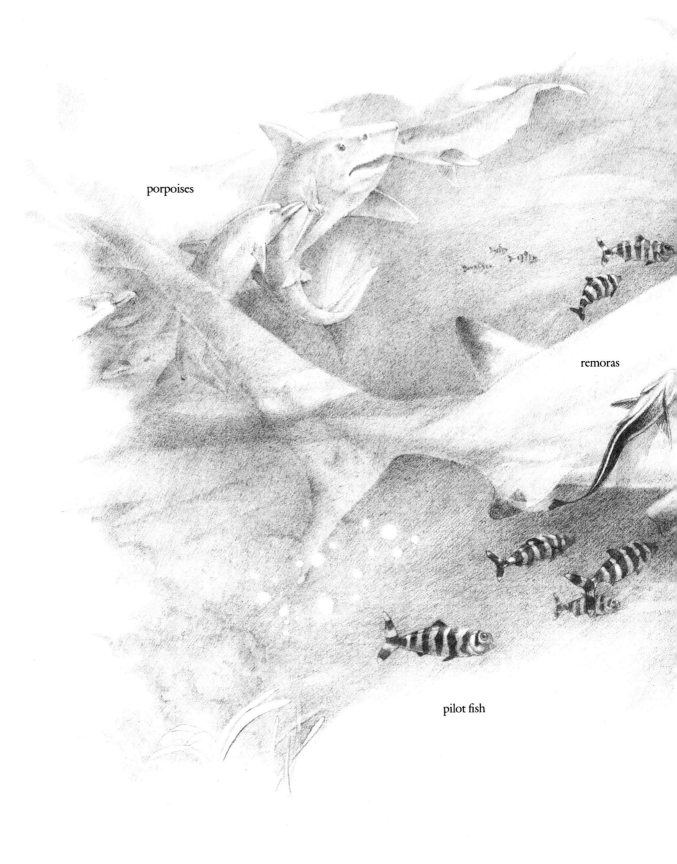

porpoises

remoras

pilot fish

blacktipped reef shark *(C. melanopterus)*

sea whips

scorpion fish

sea cucumbers

giant squid

fish, either. Porcupine fish can swell up in a shark's throat and choke it.

Some creatures challenge sharks. Swordfish and great squid fight hard to keep from being eaten by these super fish, but they often don't win. Killer whales and porpoises are more intelligent than sharks. Sometimes they win their battles with sharks and sometimes killer whales eat sharks. Porpoises will gang up on sharks that try to eat their babies. Some people have reported that a porpoise will sometimes ram a shark in the side with its hard snout. This will kill the shark, if it destroys its gills. Most sharks avoid trouble by staying away from healthy porpoises. They attack only those that are sick or too old to fight.

There is only one sea animal that kills sharks regularly. That is another shark. Big sharks eat smaller sharks. So, little sharks stay away from big sharks.

A shark's greatest enemy is man. Many people kill sharks to eat them. Some want their oil or skin. Others hunt sharks for pleasure and excitement or simply to destroy them. These people often are afraid of sharks. Actually, sharks have much more to fear from people than people do from them. People kill many more sharks than sharks kill people.

The more people learn about sharks, the more they realize that they have little to fear from them. They also realize that sharks are valuable. Sharks have an important place in the world. Like most predators, they remove sick, old, and weak animals, which helps keep the ocean clean of dead and dying creatures.

Some day we may learn that sharks are far more valuable than we ever dreamed possible. They may save millions of lives. The oil in their livers is rich in vitamin D. It is also a good medicine for treating burns. It slows down or stops the growth of some bacteria and viruses. It also stops the growth of some cancer cells.

Sharks seem to be immune to cancer. They also survive brain damage better than mammals. Researchers want to know why.

Other scientists are studying the sense organs of sharks. Some of these are much better than those of humans. Scientists think that they can use them as models for making instruments to explore the sea.

tagging a white shark in open sea

Chapter 5

Never Make a Mako Mad!

HUNDREDS OF SHARKS swim in the shallow water around islands in the Pacific. Every day children on these islands play in the water near sharks, yet the children are almost never attacked. They have been taught since they were babies to watch out for the sharks and to understand and respect them. They know that some large sharks can be dangerous. When they see one of these, they are careful.

Sometimes large sharks may mistake a person for their natural food. This does not happen often, but many things could make a shark think that an easy meal is present. To a shark, brightly colored or striped swimsuits may stand out and look like brightly colored fish. Splashing and thrashing about sends signals that sound like wounded fish. Metal objects worn by swimmers or divers may create electrical fields like those of wounded fish. Bleeding cuts, scratches, or a fisherman's speared or hooked fish send odor trails to a shark.

However, most sharks will not attack anything as large as a human. This is especially true of those that live near the shore, which would rather leave the area and look for smaller prey.

But sometimes attacks do happen. Most people who have been attacked by sharks were bitten by an angry or disturbed shark instead of a hungry one. Like dogs, most sharks do not attack unless they are provoked or feel threatened in some way. Perhaps the shark is "angry" be-

mako shark

cause a person accidentally interfered with mating. Or perhaps the person went into a nursery area where a female was laying eggs or giving birth to pups. Once in a while someone accidentally steps on a shark that is buried in the sand. Any shark might become disturbed if cornered, teased, or stepped on. A disturbed shark is dangerous. Even a little shark can give a nasty bite.

Disturbed sharks sometimes dash in and slash their tormentors with their teeth. Other times they bite once or twice and let go. Of course, the larger the shark, the nastier the bite. The razor-sharp teeth of large sharks can easily cut a blood vessel or sever an arm or leg, or even take out a large hunk of flesh. The victim may die of shock or bleed to death before getting help. Even a small bite can be serious because it may become infected. Also, the blood from the wound could bring bigger sharks.

Sometimes a disturbed shark just rams its tormentor with its snout or strikes with the edge of a pectoral fin. This can be serious, too. Deep scratches made by the rough skin teeth cause bleeding, which could attract other sharks.

Many times people are bitten because they like to show off and act silly. They try to catch a small shark with their bare hands or they grab a nurse shark by the tail. Some even try to hitch a ride on a shark's back. Usually the shark tries to get away before it turns and nips its tormentor.

Most shark bites can be avoided by using a little common sense. Anyone who looks like shark food and acts like easy prey while swimming near sharks shouldn't be surprised if he becomes the shark's dinner. Likewise, anyone who deliberately teases a shark shouldn't be surprised if he gets bitten. That is the way sharks are.

There would be fewer shark attacks if everyone treated sharks the same way they treat strange dogs. Everyone knows better than to catch, pet, or tease a strange dog. No one would think of entering a yard where a dog is growling and raising the hair on its back. A shark in its own back yard should be given the same respect.

Many sharks warn trespassers before striking. If you see a shark turning and twisting its body in an unnatural way, shaking its head, humping its body, and dropping its pectoral fins, beware. It is telling you that you are too close or have invaded its territory. And if you don't leave, you might wish you had!

The most dangerous sharks are the great white, the tiger, the bull, and the mako. Of these, the great white is the most feared. It is the largest predator and one of the most aggressive. Nothing scares a great white. It is truly the master of the sea. It is dangerous to people because it sometimes goes into shallow water.

The tiger shark is also large. It is one of the most common sharks in the tropics. It has attacked more Australians than any other shark. It, too, often comes close to shore.

The bull shark lives near the shore, but it also lives in fresh lakes and rivers. It has attacked people in both fresh water and the sea. However, most of the time, it is not dangerous.

Makos have not attacked as many people as have the great whites, but it is not wise to make a mako mad. They are the fightingest and the fastest of the sharks. Their bodies are warmer than the water they swim in. Warm muscles give them greater speed. That makes it possible for them to capture a seal or a dolphin. It also makes them more dangerous. A fifteen-foot mako bears down on its victim like a torpedo. Its compactor-like jaws could easily kill a man. Fortunately, makos don't often attack swimmers. Like all sharks, they seem to attack only those who invade their territories. Since most makos live in deep water, that seldom happens.

However, makos frequently charge boats when they are hooked. They have been known to bite holes in small boats. Some have rammed canoes with their snouts.

When caught on fishermen's hooks, makos put up a terrific fight, often leaping high into the air. Sometimes they leap into the boat! Then they cause a lot of damage to the boat and injury to the fishermen. Some bite after they seem to be dead. They may be lying quietly on the deck, but when a person comes too close, they may revive and snap their jaws just before dying. The person standing too close could receive a nasty bite.

The people in the most danger of attack are victims of crashes at sea. Blood from the injured and the splashing of panicking survivors sometimes bring a great many sharks. They may start a feeding frenzy. No one is safe if caught in a feeding frenzy.

Scientists on the United States Naval Research team were concerned about this, and looked for ways to prevent such attacks. They found that the best protection is a shark screen, a plastic bag with three inflatable rings. After the bag is filled with water, the survivor crawls in and inflates the rings. The rings keep the survivor afloat while the bag screens him from sharks. No odors of blood can reach the sharks through the plastic, and survivors do not attract sharks by thrashing around.

A great many people work and explore in the ocean. Most have never been bothered by sharks. Nonetheless, new divers are sometimes afraid of them. So scientists are searching for ways to keep sharks away from divers. They have found that a three-foot stick with sharp prongs, called a shark billy, is very useful. It can be used to push a shark away or to hit a shark on the snout. In a pinch, a camera can be used to push a shark away.

Recently scientists discovered something that may someday be even better. A milky fluid, somewhat like laundry detergent, drives sharks away and also paralyzes their jaws. This fluid was first found in the Moses sole, a small flat fish that lives in the Red Sea. Scientists hope that they can find a way to make enough of this chemical so divers could use it as a shark repellent. It could be worn in an arm band on the diver's wrist.

Perhaps the best protection is simply to learn to understand and respect sharks as do the children of the Pacific islands. People who know sharks best—those who dive among them often—do not fear them. They know from experience and observation how to behave around sharks, and have learned to respect and admire them.

There is much to admire about these very successful super fish. They are ancient survivors with special senses that most animals do not have. They are better adapted to their environment than most animals, including man.

whitetip reef shark

Moses sole

Chapter 6

A Glossary of Sharks

ALLIGATOR DOGFISH—See BRAMBLE SHARK.

AMERICAN SAWSHARK *(Pristiophorus schroederi)*—See SAWSHARKS.

ANGEL SHARKS (Squatinidae)—This is a family of sharks. There are ten known species of angel sharks. Most of them are very much alike. The flat-bodied sharks in this family look very much like skates or rays, except their winglike pectoral fins are not fastened to the head, and their five gill slits are on the side. The eyes are on top of the head, and the mouth is at the end of the snout. Angel sharks have small, tacklike teeth. They eat crabs and snails. These bottom dwellers feed mainly at night, often burrowing into the mud or sand in shallow water during the day. They are found along coasts all over the world, but are not dangerous unless stepped on or caught in nets. They are sandy gray to reddish brown on top with white bellies. Some are speckled or splotched with darker brown. An average angel shark is forty inches long. The twelve-inch pups are born alive in litters of up to sixteen. Two species are found in North American waters, the Pacific angel shark *(S. californica)* and the Atlantic angel shark *(S. dumerili)*.

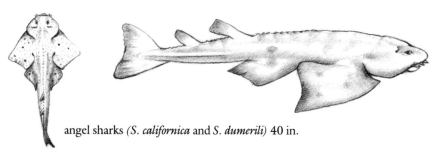

angel sharks *(S. californica* and *S. dumerili)* 40 in.

ARCTIC SHARK—See GREENLAND SHARK.

ATLANTIC ANGEL SHARK *(Squatinidae dumerili)*—See ANGEL SHARKS.

ATLANTIC SHARPNOSE SHARK *(Rhizoprionodon terraenovae)*—See SHARPNOSE SHARKS.

BASKING SHARK *(Cetorhinus maximus)*—This is the second largest of the sharks, averaging thirty feet long. It has a sharp pointed nose and small, piglike eyes. Hundreds of tiny teeth line its mouth and comblike gill rakers line the inside of its enormous gills. They eat plankton or small crustaceans. The bodies of basking sharks resemble those of the great whites. They are grayish brown to slate gray or black above, and paler underneath. The skin is studded with thornlike denticles. Basking sharks are found in cooler waters throughout the world, often seen in large groups swimming very slowly near or on the surface. During the winter they shed their gill rakers and disappear. Some scientists suggest that they hibernate on the bottom. The pups are born alive and are about five feet long.

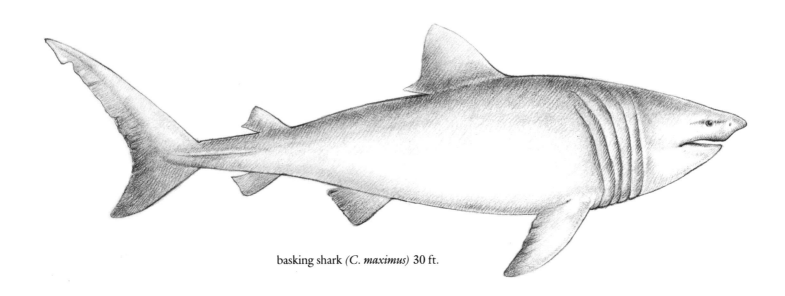

basking shark *(C. maximus)* 30 ft.

BIGEYE RAGGED-TOOTH *(Odontaspis kamohari)*—See SAND TIGER SHARK.

BIGEYE SIXGILL—See CALF SHARK.

BIGEYE THRESHER (Alopias superciliosus)—One of the three known species of the thresher shark family. *See* THRESHER SHARKS.

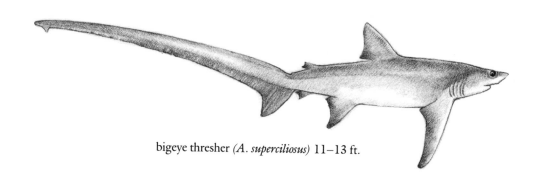

bigeye thresher *(A. superciliosus)* 11–13 ft.

BIGNOSE SHARK (Carcharhinus altimus)—This ten-foot requiem shark has a rather rounded snout. It is grayish brown on top and white underneath. Its upper teeth are triangular with serrated edges. The lower teeth are spike-like. It lives near the bottom in deep water and eats smaller sharks, squid, and octopuses. They are found in warm water of the Atlantic, Pacific, and Indian oceans. The young are born alive in litters of seven to eleven, averaging thirty inches at birth. *See also* REQUIEM SHARKS.

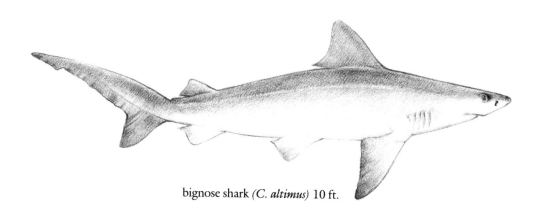

bignose shark *(C. altimus)* 10 ft.

BLACK DOGFISH (*Centroscyllium nigrum*)—This twelve-inch shark is found in deep waters of the Pacific along the coasts of California and Mexico. It eats squid, crustaceans, and jellyfish. It has very long spines on its dorsal fins, and its teeth are three-spiked. Another black dogfish (*C. fabricii*) lives in subpolar waters of the Atlantic. It has shorter spines and grows to three feet in length. *See also* DOGFISH SHARKS.

black dogfish (*C. nigrum*) 12 in.   black dogfish (*C. fabricii*) 3 ft.

BLACK WHALER—See DUSKY SHARK.

BLACKNOSE SHARK (*Carcharhinus acronotus*)—This four-foot requiem shark is found in warm water along the western Atlantic coast. It has a long snout and narrow serrated teeth. It eats small fish. These sharks are yellowish or greenish gray to brown on top and lighter in color underneath. The tip of the second dorsal fin is black and in the young there is a black blotch on the tip of the snout which fades as it gets older. They are born alive in litters of three to six and are twenty inches long at birth. *See also* REQUIEM SHARKS.

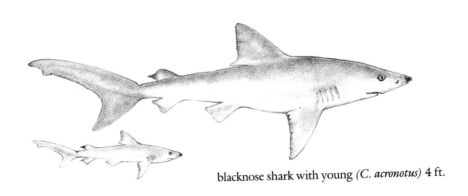

blacknose shark with young (*C. acronotus*) 4 ft.

BLACKTIP SHARK (*Carcharhinus limbatus*)—Also called small blacktip. This seven-foot requiem shark is dark gray or slate blue on top and almost white underneath. Its fins are tipped with black. It has a long conical nose and large, catlike eyes. This is an open-sea shark that frequently comes close to shore. It is common in warm waters of the Atlantic, but migrates to deeper water in winter. This active, swift-moving shark often travels in groups and feeds on squid, schooling fish, and rays. Its teeth are narrow, triangular blades with serrated edges. The twenty-four-inch young are born alive in litters of four to six pups. It is considered dangerous, but is generally shy of humans. *See also* REQUIEM SHARKS.

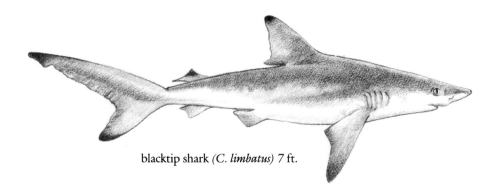

blacktip shark *(C. limbatus)* 7 ft.

BLACKTIPPED REEF SHARK (*Carcharhinus melanopterus*)—Also called blacktipped sand shark and blackfin. This six-foot requiem shark is found in shallow water in the Pacific and Indian oceans, but not in North American waters. It is gray with black-tipped fins. It eats smaller fish and is one of the few sharks known to bite prey on its first pass. It has blade-like teeth. It often travels in groups of three or four and is considered dangerous. *See also* REQUIEM SHARKS.

blacktipped reef shark *(C. melanopterus)* 6 ft.

BLAINVILLE'S DOGFISH (*Squalus blainvillei*)—This three-foot spiny dog-
fish lives in the eastern Pacific. *See* DOGFISH SHARKS.

Blainville's dogfish *(S. blainvillei)* 3 ft.

BLUE POINTER—Same as shortfin mako. *See* MAKO SHARKS.

BLUE SHARK (*Prionace glauca*)—This eight- to twelve-foot requiem shark is among
the most beautiful of all sharks. Its slim body is deep blue with a snow-
white belly. It has a long pointed snout, a long tail, and very long curved
pectoral fins. The dorsal fin is near the middle of the back. Its eyes are
large and rimmed with white. Blue sharks have serrated, triangular upper teeth and spikelike lowers. They eat schooling fish, squid, and injured whales, and pursue their prey for great distances. They can travel
at least thirty miles per hour. Blue sharks live far from shore in all tem-
perate and tropical seas. In summer, they swim near the surface and in
deeper water in winter. The pups are born alive in litters of twenty-five
to fifty, averaging eighteen inches long. *See also* REQUIEM SHARKS.

blue shark *(P. glauca)* 8–12 ft.

BONITO SHARK—Same as shortfin mako. *See* MAKO SHARKS.

BONNETHEAD SHARK *(Sphyrna tiburo)*—Also called shovelhead. This 3.5-foot hammerhead has a rounded, shovel-shaped head. It is grayish brown with a paler stomach. It lives in warm water in the Atlantic, mostly in shallow water, and feeds on shrimp, crabs, mollusks, and small fish. Its teeth are sharp and bladelike. It is often seen in groups of ten to twenty and sometimes hundreds. It migrates south in winter or to deeper offshore water. The young are born alive in litters of eight to twelve. They are about a foot long at birth. *See also* HAMMERHEAD SHARKS.

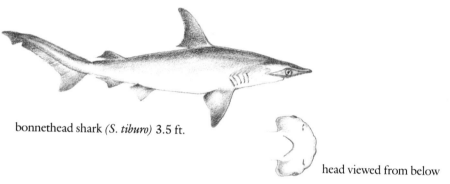

bonnethead shark *(S. tiburo)* 3.5 ft.

head viewed from below

BRAMBLE SHARK *(Echinorhinus brucus)*—Also called spiny shark and alligator dogfish. This nine-foot dogfish is dark gray or brown to black on top, and is often covered with darker blotches. Its belly is paler. Large spiked denticles are widely spaced over its body. The first dorsal fin is set far back, near the tail. Its teeth have several smooth-edged points. It lives in very deep water around the world and is not often found in North American waters. It is born alive in litters of twenty-four pups, and is about sixteen inches at birth. *See also* DOGFISH SHARKS.

bramble shark *(E. brucus)* 9 ft.

BRONZE WHALER—*See* NARROWTOOTH SHARK.

BROWN CATSHARK (*Apristurus brunneus*)—This two-foot-long brown catshark is found along the Pacific coast of North America. It has a long snout and small dorsal fins. The first dorsal is set far back, near the second. The fins are edged with black. The teeth have five smooth-edged, needle-sharp points. It lives in deep water and feeds on shrimp and small fish. The young hatch from eggs and are about three inches long when hatched. *See also* CATSHARKS.

brown catshark (*A. brunneus*) 2 ft.

BROWN SMOOTHHOUND SHARK (*Mustelus henlei*)—This 2.5-foot brown shark has a silvery white belly. It has a pointed snout, and its dorsal fins are usually frayed along the rear edges. Its teeth are small, pavement-like, and have short, sharp points. It eats crabs, shrimp, and small fish. This shark is found in shallow water, usually very close to shore along the California coast. It is one of the most often found in San Francisco Bay. The eight-inch young are born alive. *See also* SMOOTH-HOUND SHARKS.

brown smoothhound shark (*M. henlei*) 2.5 ft.

BULL SHARK *(Carcharhinus leucas)*—This ten-foot requiem shark has a very short, rounded snout; a large first dorsal fin; and long, pointed pectoral fins. It is grayish on top and white underneath. The fins are black-tipped in the young. These sluggish, shallow-water sharks live in all warm seas along coasts and near the mouths of rivers. Some live in fresh water, swimming hundreds of miles upstream. Others live in freshwater lakes. These are often called by the name of the area they inhabit; for example, the one living in the Zambezi River is called the Zambezi shark. Bull sharks are found along all coasts of North America. Their serrated upper teeth are large and broadly triangular. The lower teeth are spikelike. Bull sharks eat other sharks, rays, fish, mollusks, and crustaceans. The young are born alive and are twenty-nine inches long. Bull sharks are dangerous and have been known to attack humans. *See also* REQUIEM SHARKS.

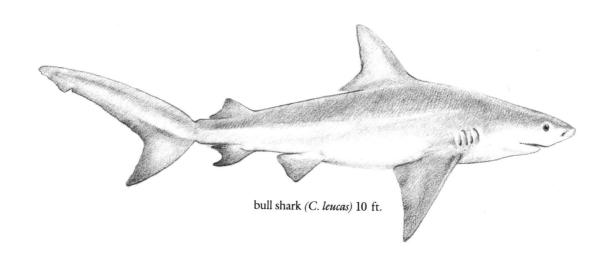

bull shark *(C. leucas)* 10 ft.

BULLHEAD SHARKS (Heterodontidae)—Also called horn sharks and Port Jackson sharks. This is a family of sharks. Eight species are known. They are found in the Pacific and Indian oceans. They have two large dorsal fins equipped with strong spines on the front edge. They have blunt snouts, ridges over the eyes, and grooves on the upper and lower lips. They range in size from twenty-eight to thirty-six inches. They have pointed grasping teeth in front for seizing prey, and flat molars in back for crushing oysters, crabs, and other shellfish. They eat at night and are found near the bottom in deep water. Bullhead sharks hatch from brown, screw-shaped eggs. Only two species are found in North American waters: the horn shark (*H. francisci*) and the Mexican horn shark (*H. mexicanus*). The Port Jackson shark (*H. portusjacksoni*) is found near Australia.

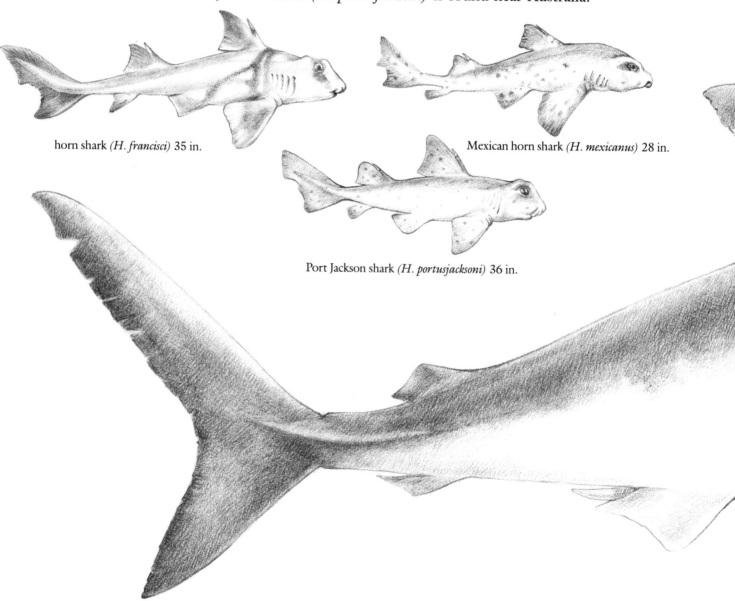

horn shark (*H. francisci*) 35 in.

Mexican horn shark (*H. mexicanus*) 28 in.

Port Jackson shark (*H. portusjacksoni*) 36 in.

CALF SHARK (*Hexanchus vitulus*)—Also known as bigeye sixgill shark. This seven-foot cow shark has six gill slits, only one dorsal fin, and large, bright green eyes. It is dark gray on top and lighter in color underneath. The upper teeth of this fish-eater are long and pointed. The lower teeth are large, broad, and sawlike. This deepwater shark lives throughout the world and is found around Florida. The young are born alive, thirteen pups per litter, and are sixteen inches at birth. *See also* COWSHARKS.

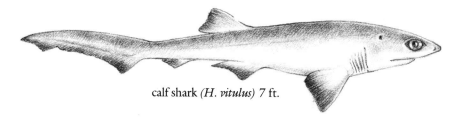

calf shark *(H. vitulus)* 7 ft.

CARCHARODON MEGALODON—This was a prehistoric shark. It is known only from fossil teeth and impressions left in rock. It was probably the largest shark that ever lived. One of its teeth was over five inches long. The tooth is very similar to those of its close relative, the great white shark. It may have been forty-three feet long.

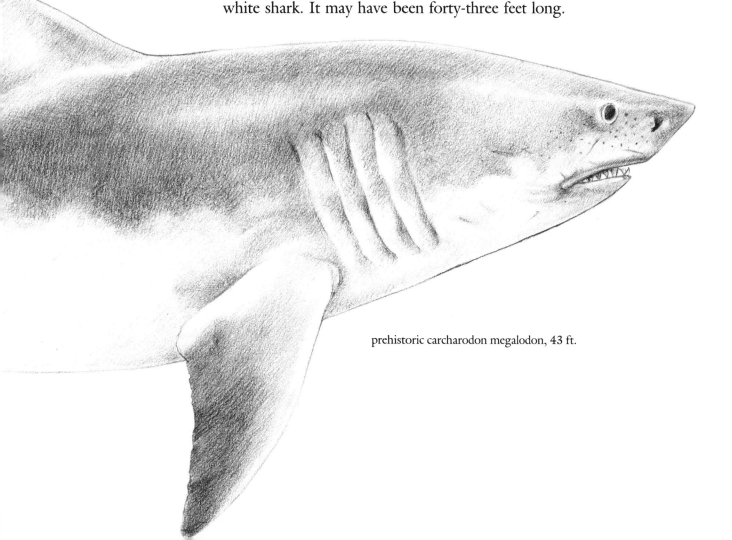

prehistoric carcharodon megalodon, 43 ft.

CARIBBEAN REEF SHARK—See REEF SHARK.

CARIBBEAN SHARPNOSE SHARK *(Rhizoprionodon porosus)*—See SHARPNOSE SHARKS.

CARPET SHARKS (Ginglymostomatidae)—Also called nurse sharks. This is a family of broad-bodied, bottom-dwelling sharks. They include the wobbegongs and nurse sharks. These sharks are six to ten feet long. They are very sluggish and often lie motionless in warm shallow water close to the shore. Some are beautifully colored and patterned. Others are dull grays. All have fleshy barbels, or feelers, on their snouts just in front of the mouth and a deep groove connects the nostrils and mouth. Their snouts are short and their eyes are small. Carpet sharks have five gills, but look as if they have only four. The fifth gill is very small and is almost covered by the fourth. Carpet sharks eat invertebrates and small fish. Some are born alive, others hatch from eggs. At least twelve species are known, but only the nurse shark is found in North American waters. They are harmless unless provoked.

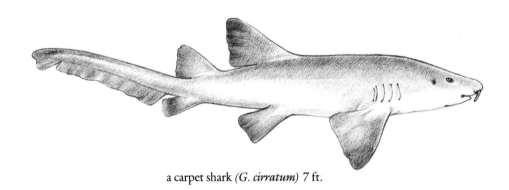

a carpet shark *(G. cirratum)* 7 ft.

CATSHARKS (Scyliorhinidae)—This is a large family of small (two to three feet), bottom-dwelling sharks. Eighty-six species are known. They live all over the world, mostly in deep cool coastal waters. They have short broad pectoral fins, large oval eyes, and small teeth. Many are patterned, striped, or spotted. Most hatch from eggs, but a few are born alive. Only eighteen species are found in North American waters. Many do not have common names. The chain dogfish, head shark, marbled catshark, and swell shark are in this family.

catshark *(S. boa)* 2 ft.

CHAIN DOGFISH *(Scyliorhinus retifer)*—In spite of its name, this shark is not a dogfish. It is a small catshark, with a slender fifteen-inch body, a wedge-shaped snout, and bright green eyes. Its small triangular teeth have three points, one long and two short. It is ivory to reddish brown in color with dark brown, chainlike markings on its back and sides. This bottom dweller lives in cool, deep offshore water along the Atlantic coast of North America. It hatches from small, rectangular eggs. Newly hatched pups are about four inches long. *See also* CATSHARKS.

chain dogfish *(S. retifer)* 15 in.

COCKTAIL SHARK *(Carcharhinus greyi)*—Also called bronze whaler. This small requiem shark may be the same species as the dusky shark. It is bronze in color and up to thirteen feet long. It lives off southern Australia. *See also* REQUIEM SHARKS.

cocktail shark *(C. greyi)* 12–13 ft.

COMMON THRESHER *(Alopias vulpinus)*—One of three known species of the thresher shark family. *See* THRESHER SHARKS.

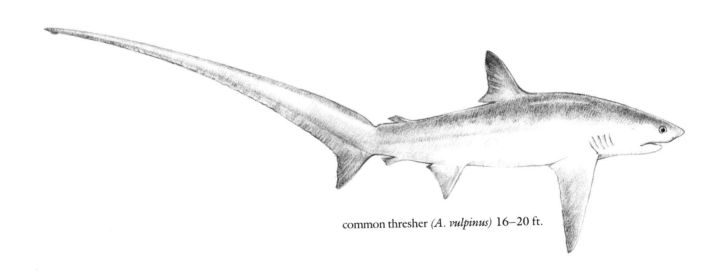

common thresher *(A. vulpinus)* 16–20 ft.

COOKIE-CUTTER SHARK *(Isistius brasiliensis)*—Also called luminous shark.

This small dogfish shark averages about a foot long. It has two spineless dorsal fins of equal size set far back on its body. The body is a dark grayish brown on top and lighter in color underneath, with a dark collar around the neck. The body fins are tipped with white, and the tail fins are tipped with black. Its underside is covered with luminous organs which give off a greenish light that glows in the dark. Its mouth is circular and filled with sharp, pointed upper teeth and very large, knifelike lower teeth. The lower teeth are interlocked, giving them extra strength. This shark lives in large groups in warm, deep waters all around the world. It migrates to upper waters at night where it waits for prey—large squid, whales, porpoises, or tuna. When one comes along, it dashes in and grabs hold with its razor-sharp teeth and twists. It swims away with a bite of flesh, leaving a perfectly round hole in its victim. These sharks are born alive, five or six at a time. *See also* DOGFISH SHARKS.

cookie-cutter shark *(I. brasiliensis)* 12 in.

COWSHARK—See SIXGILL SHARK.

COWSHARKS (Hexanchidae)—This is a shark family. Only four species are known: the calf shark, sixgill shark, sevengill shark, and the sharpnose sevengill. These sharks have six or seven gills, slender bodies, and only one dorsal fin. These are the most primitive of the sharks and look more like their ancestors than any other of the living sharks.

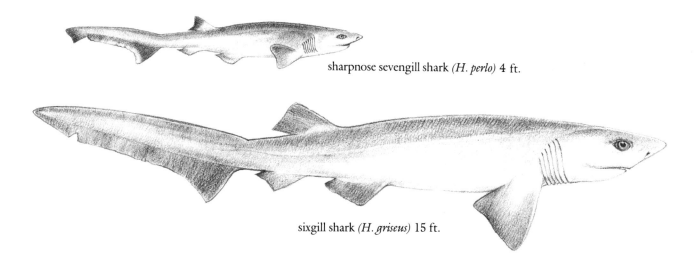

sharpnose sevengill shark *(H. perlo)* 4 ft.

sixgill shark *(H. griseus)* 15 ft.

CUBAN RIBBONTAIL CATSHARK *(Eridacnis barbouri)*—See RIBBONTAIL CATSHARKS.

DEEPWATER CATSHARK *(Apristurus profundorum)*—This small grayish brown or black catshark is found in deep water of the Atlantic. This two-foot long shark has a broad snout. Its first dorsal fin is located far back over the pelvic fin. *See also* CATSHARKS.

deepwater catshark *(A. profundorum)* 2 ft.

DEVIL FISH SHARK *(Etmopterus lucifer)*—Also called dwarf shark. This small dogfish has large eyes. It grows to be twelve inches long. Its body is grayish with lighter colored tail fins and has lines of luminous organs on its sides. Its upper teeth have several points, the lower only one. This shark is found in deep ocean waters near Japan. It eats squid and octopuses which it hunts in packs, often attacking prey larger than itself. *See also* DOGFISH SHARKS.

devil fish shark *(E. lucifer)* 12 in.

DOGFISH SHARKS (Squalidae)—This is a large family of sharks. There are at least seventy-six different species, twenty-six of them found in North American waters. Many are quite similar, and many have no common names. They range in size from six inches to twenty feet long. Most are small. All have streamlined bodies and two dorsal fins but no anal fins. Some have sharp, thornlike spines on the front edge of their dorsal fins, which may be poisonous. Most have small, smoothedged teeth. Their color varies. Some are gray, some are brown, and many are black. Many are luminous and have large eyes. They live in cool or deep waters in all oceans. Some live in icy polar water. Dogfish are born alive. They are not dangerous to humans. Scientists often use them for research.

DUSKY SHARK (*Carcharhinus obscurus*)—Also called black whaler. This twelve-foot requiem shark is found inshore and offshore in all warm and temperate oceans. It has a ridged back and is gray or bluish gray on top and white underneath. Its jaws are powerful and lined with serrated cutting teeth in the upper jaw and narrow, spikelike holding teeth below. It eats almost anything—fish, sharks, rays, eels, squid, octopuses, and starfish. Dusky sharks migrate north in summer and south in winter. The young are born alive near the shore in litters of six to fourteen. They are about thirty-six inches long. These sharks are big enough and plentiful enough to be considered dangerous, but are not especially aggressive. *See also* REQUIEM SHARKS.

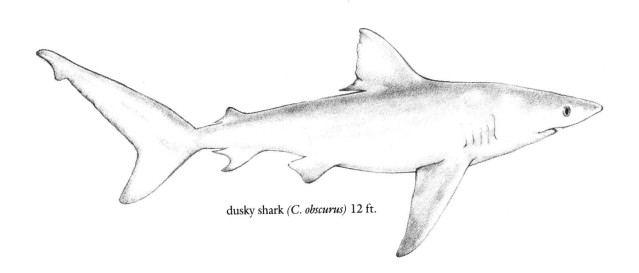

dusky shark *(C. obscurus)* 12 ft.

DWARF SHARK—See DEVIL FISH SHARK.

FALSE CATSHARK *(Pseudotriakis microdon)*—This rare deepwater shark is found in both the Atlantic and Pacific oceans. It has a short, pointed snout; tiny teeth; and a very long, low first dorsal fin set near the center of its slender ten-foot body. This dark brown shark belongs to the Pseudo-triakidae family. Its two pups are born alive when they are nearly one yard long.

false catshark *(P. microdon)* 10 ft.

FILETAIL CATSHARK *(Parmaturus xaniurus)*—This small, twenty-inch cat-shark is found in deep water off the coast of California. It has a short snout and pointed teeth. The first dorsal fin sets far back. A row of en-larged skin teeth line the upper edge of its tail. It is brownish white on top and lighter in color underneath. The pups hatch from slender, four-inch-long eggs. *See also* CATSHARKS.

filetail catshark *(P. xaniurus)* 20 in.

FINETOOTH SHARK *(Carcharhinus isodon)*—This requiem shark grows to six feet in length. It has a short snout; smooth-edged, spikelike teeth; and a large first dorsal fin. It eats small fish. This shark is slate blue on top and white underneath. It is found in shallow tropical waters along the Atlantic coast and the Gulf of Mexico. Its nineteen-inch pups are born alive. *See also* REQUIEM SHARKS.

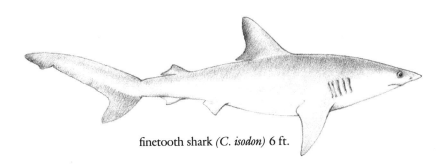

finetooth shark *(C. isodon)* 6 ft.

FLORIDA DOGFISH SHARK *(Mustelus norrisi)*—Also called Florida smoothhound. This 3.5-foot smoothhound is found in shallow coastal waters from Florida to Brazil. Its slender body is grayish brown on top and dirty white underneath. It has a large second dorsal fin and small, molarlike teeth. This shark eats crabs, shrimp, and small fish. The twelve-inch pups are born alive in litters of seven to fourteen. *See also* SMOOTHHOUND SHARKS.

Florida dogfish shark *(M. norrisi)* 3.5 ft.

FRILLED SHARK *(Chlamydoselachus anguineus)*—This is the only member of the
frilled shark family. It is found in deep water around the world. It has a
six-foot, brownish gray, snakelike body. Its mouth is at the end of its
snout. It has six gills. The gill covers are frilled and the first one circles
the throat. The single dorsal fin is near the tail. Its teeth have five spikes,
and it eats octopuses and squid. The twenty-inch pups are born alive in
litters of up to twelve.

frilled shark *(C. anguineus)* 6 ft.

GALÁPAGOS SHARK *(Carcharhinus galapagensis)*—This twelve-foot gray-brown
requiem shark has a cream belly. It resembles the dusky, but has a larger,
more pointed dorsal fin and smaller gill slits. It is found in deep water
along the shores of most tropical Pacific islands during the day, going
into shallower water at dusk. It eats fish, eels, octopuses, and squid. The
upper teeth are triangular, the lower spikelike. The thirty-one-inch pups
are born alive, nine to sixteen per litter. *See also* REQUIEM SHARKS.

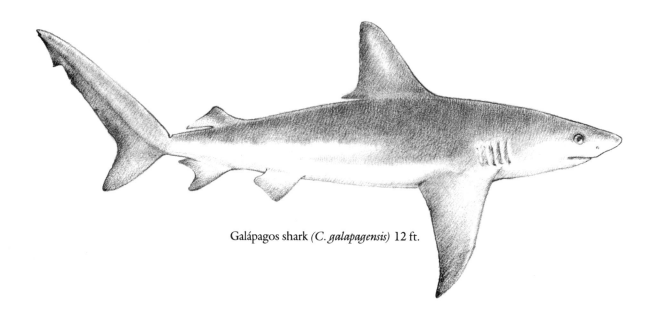

Galápagos shark *(C. galapagensis)* 12 ft.

GANGES RIVER SHARK *(Carcharhinus gangeticus)*—This large requiem shark is probably the same as the bull shark. It lives in rivers along the Indian Ocean and in Japan. It has attacked bathers in the Ganges River. *See also* BULL SHARK and REQUIEM SHARKS.

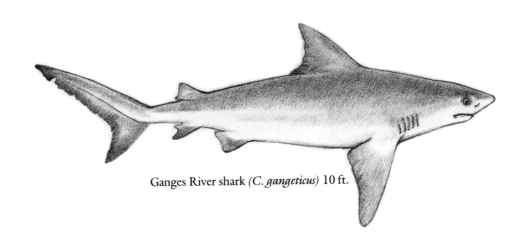

Ganges River shark *(C. gangeticus)* 10 ft.

GOBLIN SHARK *(Scapanorhynchus owstoni)*—This deepwater shark is the only species in the goblin shark family. It is unlike any other. It has a long, shovel-like snout and round fins. Little is known about this rare shark that lives in the deep oceans. Its fifteen-foot body is gray, white, or pinkish. It probably eats small prey, because it has spikelike front teeth and tiny rear teeth.

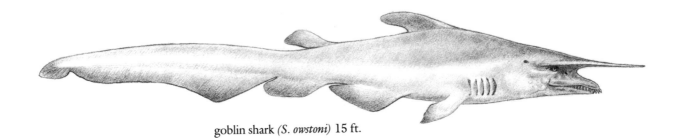

goblin shark *(S. owstoni)* 15 ft.

GRAY NURSE SHARK *(Odontaspis arenarius)*—See SAND TIGER SHARK.

GRAY REEF SHARK *(Carcharhinus amblyrhynchos)*—This seven-foot requiem shark lives along the Indo-Pacific reefs. It is light gray with a black margin on the tail. It has triangular, bladelike teeth and eats fish. This shark displays warning signals before it attacks. Its twenty-inch pups are born alive in litters of six to eleven. This shark is considered dangerous. The common Red Sea gray reef shark *(C. wheeleri)* is closely related to this shark. *See also* REQUIEM SHARKS.

gray reef shark *(C. amblyrhynchos)* 7 ft.

GRAY SHARKS—See REQUIEM SHARKS.

GRAY SMOOTHHOUND SHARK *(Mustelus californicus)*—This five-foot slender-bodied shark is found near the shores of California. It is a medium gray, white-bellied shark with a fairly large second dorsal fin. Its teeth are rounded and molar-shaped for crushing crabs and other hard-shelled sea animals. Its twelve-inch pups are born alive in litters of three to sixteen. *See also* SMOOTHHOUND SHARKS.

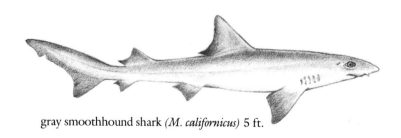

gray smoothhound shark *(M. californicus)* 5 ft.

GREAT HAMMERHEAD *(Sphyrna mokarran)*—See HAMMERHEAD SHARKS.

GREAT WHITE SHARK *(Carcharodon carcharias)*—Also called white pointer.
This shark is the largest and most dangerous predatory shark. This large mackerel shark is the most talked about and the least known of all large animals. It is fourteen to twenty-one feet long and is heavily built. It lives offshore in both cool and warm seas all over the world. It sometimes wanders into shallow water. Its snout is conical, its eyes are black, and the tail lobes are almost equal in size. Its second dorsal fin is very small. This shark has large triangular serrated teeth. It is dirty brownish gray on top and dirty white underneath, often with black spots at the base of the pectoral fins. It is a fast swimmer because its body is warmer than the sea water. It eats large animals—seals, sea lions, porpoises, tuna, sea turtles, whales, and other sharks as well as crabs. Its pups are born alive and are about four feet long. It has attacked more swimmers than any other shark, but usually avoids divers. *See also* MACKEREL SHARKS.

great white shark *(C. carcharias)* 14–21 ft.

GREEN DOGFISH *(Etmopterus virens)*—This deepwater shark is ten to twelve inches long and is found in the Gulf of Mexico. The second dorsal fin is larger than the first and both have spines at the base. It is a dark sooty brown with two pale blue-gray stripes on each side and a yellowish spot on the head. Its belly glows a bright green like a firefly, which may help it stay with others in large schools. The upper teeth have four or five points; the lower only one with a flat cutting edge. It eats squid and octopuses. The four-inch pups are born alive, one to three at a time. *See also* DOG-FISH SHARKS.

green dogfish *(E. virens)* 10–12 in.

GREENLAND SHARK *(Somniosus microcephalus)*—Also called sleeper shark or arctic shark. This huge, spineless dogfish, up to twenty-one feet long, is often found on the bottom in very deep and cold polar waters of the North Atlantic. Its dorsal fins are nearly equal in size. The first is about midway down the back. Greenland sharks are coffee brown to ash gray in color. Their upper teeth are spikelike and their lower are bladelike. They eat fish and seals, and give birth to ten to sixteen pups that are fifteen inches long. *See also* DOGFISH SHARKS.

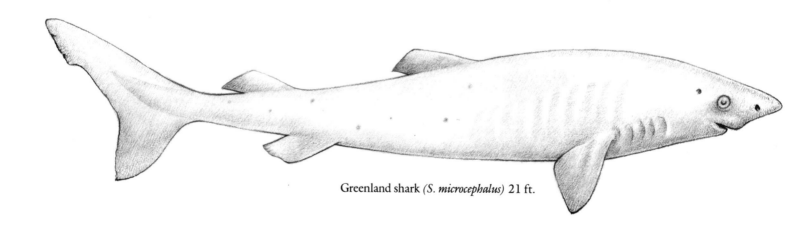

Greenland shark *(S. microcephalus)* 21 ft.

GULPER SHARK *(Centrophorus granulosus)* —This five-foot, deepwater dogfish is found in the Gulf of Mexico, most of the Atlantic, and the Mediterranean. It has spines at the base of its two dorsal fins and pointed trailing edges on the pectoral fins. The first dorsal fin is mid-back. It is dark gray or brown on top and lighter in color underneath. The upper teeth are smooth and triangular; the lower have slanting points and are finely serrated. It is not known what they eat. Its four to six pups are fourteen inches long at birth. *See also* DOGFISH SHARKS.

gulper shark *(C. granulosus)* 5 ft.

HAMMERHEAD SHARKS (Sphyrnidae)—This is a family of sharks. There are six known species. All of them have wide, flat heads. These very advanced sharks are found along coasts in warm seas all over the world. (The scalloped hammerhead forms huge schools in warmer water.) They range in size from three to twenty feet long. Their color varies from dark olive to brownish gray. Their rudderlike heads may help them swim faster and dive deeper. They may also improve the senses of smell and sight. The eyes are located at the tip of the long lobes which may be a yard wide. The nostrils are on the front edge, and in some they are two feet

apart. Hammerheads swim constantly, sometimes swinging their heads from side to side. There are a large number of ampullae of Lorenzini on the bottom of the head. Hammerheads may use their heads like mine sweepers to find stingrays, their favorite food, buried in the sand. These sharks also eat fish and other sharks. They have bladelike teeth and can be dangerous. They are born alive. The young of the great hammerhead (the largest of the hammerheads) are twenty-eight inches long when born. The common or smooth hammerhead has litters of twenty to forty pups that are twenty inches long. The most common kinds found in North American waters are the great hammerhead *(Sphyrna mokarran)*, the scalloped hammerhead *(S. lewini)*, the common or smooth hammerhead *(S. zygaena)*, the scoophead *(S. media)*, the smalleye hammerhead *(S. tudes)*, and the bonnethead shark *(S. tiburo)*. They are all very similar except for the size and shape of their hammer-like heads.

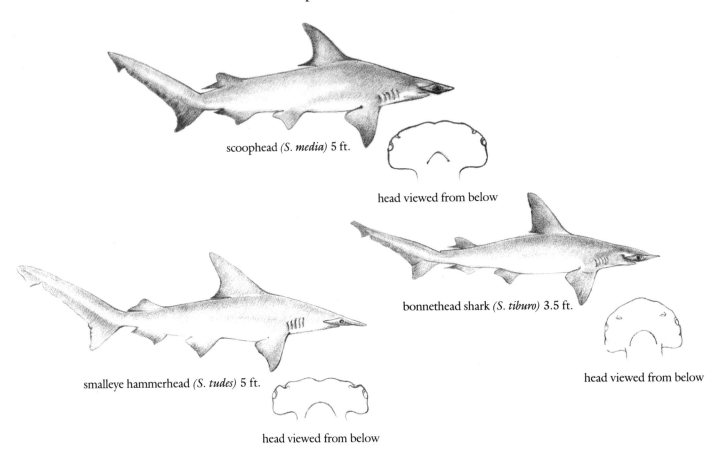

scoophead *(S. media)* 5 ft.

head viewed from below

bonnethead shark *(S. tiburo)* 3.5 ft.

head viewed from below

smalleye hammerhead *(S. tudes)* 5 ft.

head viewed from below

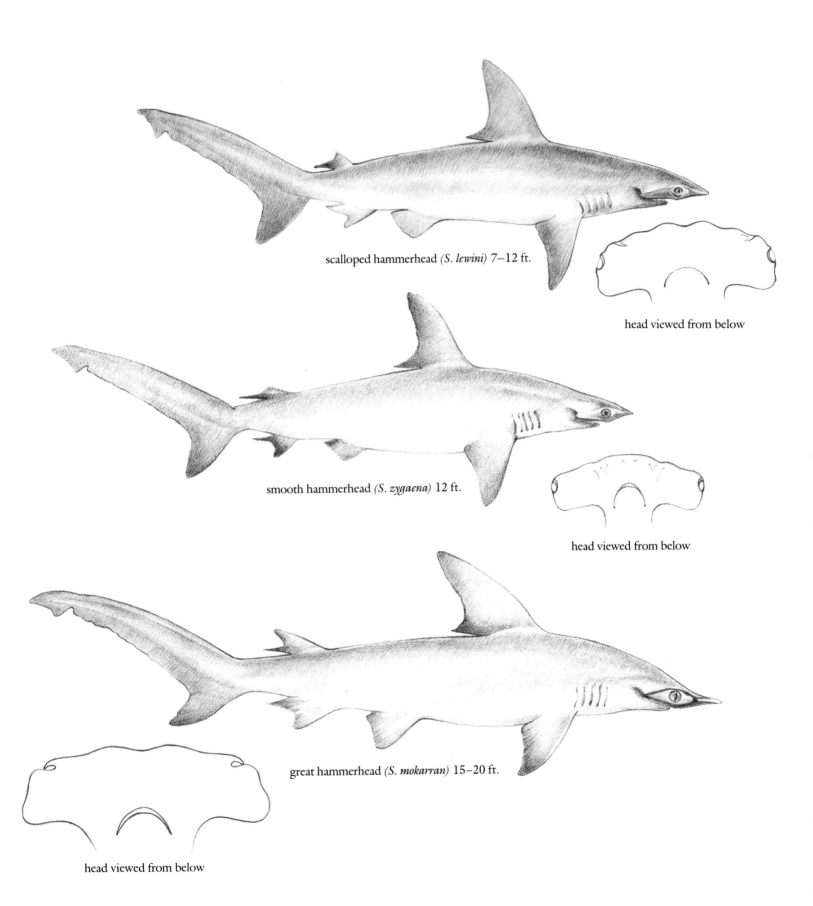

scalloped hammerhead *(S. lewini)* 7–12 ft.

head viewed from below

smooth hammerhead *(S. zygaena)* 12 ft.

head viewed from below

great hammerhead *(S. mokarran)* 15–20 ft.

head viewed from below

HEAD SHARK *(Cephalurus cephalus)*—This seven- to fourteen-inch catshark swims in schools in deep water in the Gulf of California. This shark looks as if it were all head, because the gill slits, pectoral fins, and dorsal fins are set far back on the body. The dorsal fins are nearly equal in size. It is dark gray, brown, or blackish on top and lighter in color underneath. It has green eyes. The wide flattened head has a very short, rounded snout. The teeth are small, smooth-edged, and three-pointed. The four-inch pups are born alive. *See also* CATSHARKS.

head shark *(C. cephalus)* 7–14 in.

HORN SHARKS—See BULLHEAD SHARKS.

INSHORE WHITETIP—See SILVERTIP SHARK.

KITEFIN SHARK *(Dalatias licha)*—This six-foot, dark gray or chocolate brown dogfish has spineless dorsal fins. The first dorsal fin is set nearer the head than in most dogfish. It lives in moderately deep water in the northern Atlantic. Its upper teeth are spikelike and the lower are triangular and serrated. It eats fish, rays, crabs, and squid. Its twelve-inch pups are born alive in litters of ten to sixteen. *See also* DOGFISH SHARKS.

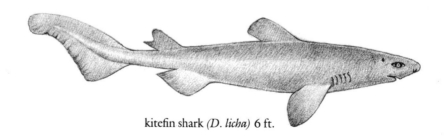

kitefin shark *(D. licha)* 6 ft.

LANTERN SHARKS *(Etmopterus)*—This is a group of small spiny dogfish sharks. They have luminous bellies that glow in the dark like fireflies. These foot-long sharks live on the ocean floor in very deep tropical water. They eat squid and shrimplike creatures. *See also* DOGFISH SHARKS.

(E. hillianus) 10–13 in.

(E. bullisi) 7–9 in.

(E. gracilispinis) 12 in.

(E. schultzi) 12 in.

LARGE BLACKTIP SHARK—See SPINNER SHARK.

LEMON SHARK (*Negaprion brevirostris*)—This eleven-foot night feeding requiem shark is found in warm waters near the shore or river mouths along both coasts of North America. In the daytime it is found in deeper water, sometimes resting on the bottom. It has a short, wide snout, and its two dorsal fins are nearly equal in size. It is yellowish brown or olive gray on top and yellowish underneath. Its teeth are narrowly triangular with finely serrated bases. It eats fish, rays, shrimp, crabs, small sharks, and sea birds. The twenty-four-inch pups are born alive, averaging eleven per litter. This shark is not aggressive, but could be dangerous. *See also* REQUIEM SHARKS.

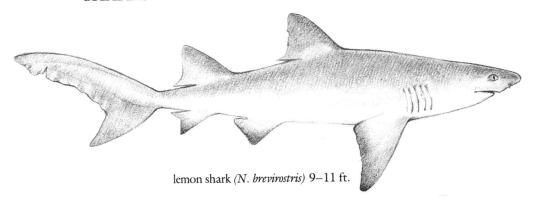

lemon shark *(N. brevirostris)* 9–11 ft.

LEOPARD SHARK (*Triakis semifasciata*)—This five- to six-foot smoothhound is grayish brown on top with dark markings or bars and spots, and sometimes stripes, along the back. Large groups of these sharks are found in shallow water along the Pacific coast of the United States. They have a great many small, spiked teeth. They eat crabs, shrimp, clams, octopuses, small fish, and fish eggs. The eight-inch pups are born alive in litters of seven to thirty. *See also* SMOOTHHOUND SHARKS.

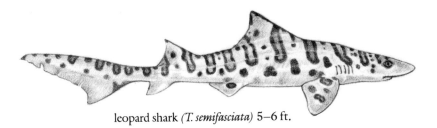

leopard shark *(T. semifasciata)* 5–6 ft.

LONGFIN MAKO *(Isurus paucus)*—One of the two species of makos. *See* MAKO SHARKS.

LONGNOSE CATSHARK *(Apristurus kampae)*—This rare deep-ocean cat-shark is known only from two specimens. It is fourteen inches long. It has a long snout and short pectoral fins. Its long slender body is dark gray or black. It eats shrimp, and its pups hatch from eggs. *See also* CAT-SHARKS.

longnose catshark *(A. kampae)* 14 in.

LUMINOUS SHARK—See COOKIE-CUTTER SHARK and LANTERN SHARKS.

MACKEREL SHARKS (Lamnidae)—Also called porbeagles. This is a family of large, fast-swimming sharks. There are five known species: the great white, shortfin mako, longfin mako, salmon shark, and porbeagle shark. These sharks are the most powerful, the most graceful, and the most dangerous of all sharks. They have streamlined bodies, pointed snouts, very large gills, very small second dorsal fins, and nearly equal upper and lower lobes of the tail. They range from eight to twenty-one feet in length and are found offshore in deep waters throughout the world. Some are warm-blooded. The sharks in this family are called mackerel sharks because they eat mackerel fish. They also eat salmon, tuna, swordfish, sharks, seals, and sea lions. The pups are born alive.

a mackerel shark *(L. nasus)* 8 ft.

MAKO SHARKS

MAKO SHARKS—There are two kinds of mako sharks, the longfin mako *(Isurus paucus)*, and the more common, shortfin mako *(Isurus oxyrinchus)*, which is also sometimes called the bonito, the blue pointer, or the sharpnose mackerel shark. Makos are members of the mackerel shark family. They are among the most beautiful of the sharks. The two species look very much alike, except that the longfin mako has such longer pectoral fins, larger eyes, and sometimes a yellowish belly. The shortfin has a snowy white belly. Both are deep blue on top. The eyes are black. Makos range from ten to thirteen feet long. These sharks are the fastest swimmers and the highest leapers of all sharks. Their warm blood, slender bodies, and very sharp snouts enable them to reach speeds of forty miles per hour. They sometimes leap twenty feet above the water. The upper lobes of the tail are nearly equal in size, and the second dorsal fin is very small. Their teeth are finger-shaped, razor sharp, long, and pointed. They eat all kinds of fish, even the broadbill swordfish, which is rarely eaten by other animals. Their food is swallowed whole. Makos are found in warm and cool waters throughout the world. They swim mostly in deep water, only occasionally going into shallow water. The twenty-five to twenty-seven-inch pups are born alive in litters of eight to ten. These sharks are considered to be one of the most dangerous types of shark. They are very aggressive and when hooked, sometimes charge boats. *See also* MACKEREL SHARKS.

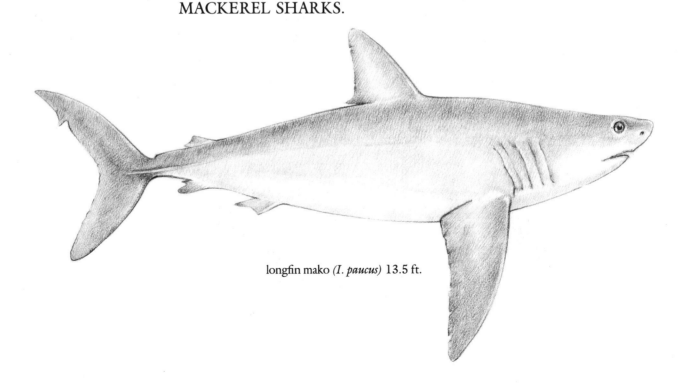

longfin mako *(I. paucus)* 13.5 ft.

MARBLED CATSHARK (Galeus arae)—This fourteen- to eighteen-inch catshark is found in warm water off Florida and the Gulf of Mexico. The adults live in deep water, the young in shallower water. Its slender body is pale yellowish brown with dark brown blotches and spots on the back and sides. The dorsal fins are small and nearly equal in size; the first is set far back. The lower tail lobe is very small. This shark has sharp, three-pointed teeth. It eats deepwater shrimp. It is believed that they are born alive. *See also* CATSHARKS.

marbled catshark (*G. arae*) 14–18 in.

MEGAMOUTH SHARK (Megachasma pelagios)—One of the most recently discovered species, this fifteen-foot shark is known from only two specimens. The first one was found entangled in a sea anchor of a navy research ship in deep water off Hawaii. Like the whale shark's, the mouth of this shark is at the end of its snout. Gill rakers line its gills and tiny teeth line its jaws. But in megamouth, there appears to be luminescent tissue inside its mouth that may lure plankton and deep sea shrimp into its enormous jaws. This shark is dark slate gray on top and lighter in color underneath. Little else is known about this very unusual shark.

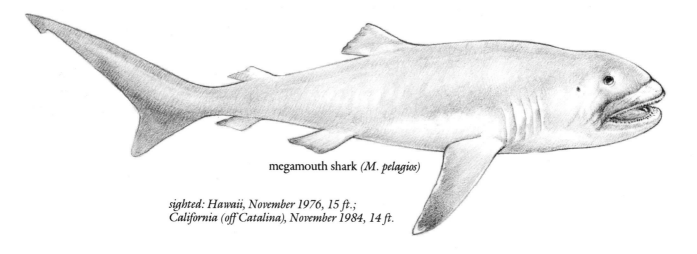

megamouth shark (*M. pelagios*)

sighted: Hawaii, November 1976, 15 ft.;
California (off Catalina), November 1984, 14 ft.

MEXICAN HORN SHARK *(Heterodontus mexicanus)*—See BULLHEAD SHARKS.

MUD SHARK—See SIXGILL SHARK.

NARROWTOOTH SHARK *(Carcharhinus brachyurus)*—Also called bronze
whaler in Australia. This 9.5-foot requiem shark is found in warm waters throughout the world. It has a long snout, large first dorsal and small second dorsal fins, and triangular to scythelike teeth which are finely serrated. It is mousy or brownish gray on top and lighter in color underneath, with dark edges on the fins. It feeds on bottom-dwelling fish. Its thirteen to twenty pups are born alive and are about twenty-five inches long. This shark may be dangerous. *See also* REQUIEM SHARKS.

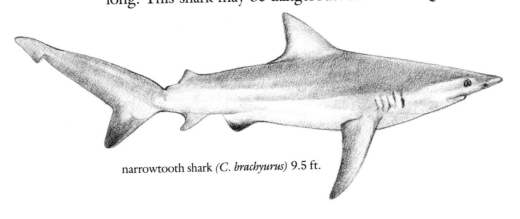

narrowtooth shark *(C. brachyurus)* 9.5 ft.

NIGHT SHARK *(Carcharhinus signatus)*—This seven-foot requiem shark is bluish
gray with black spots on top and lighter in color underneath. It is found along the east coast of North America, in the Gulf of Mexico, and along the west coast of Africa. It prefers warm, deep water but goes into shallow waters at dusk. This shark has a long snout, green eyes, and a relatively small first dorsal fin. Its teeth are serrated; the uppers are triangular and the lowers are spikelike. It eats fish and shrimp. The twenty-eight-inch pups are born alive in litters of twelve to eighteen. *See also* REQUIEM SHARKS.

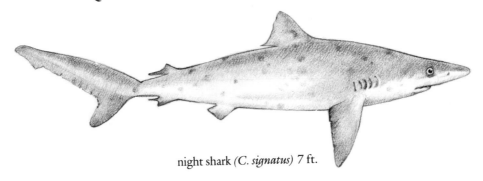

night shark *(C. signatus)* 7 ft.

NURSE SHARK *(Ginglymostoma cirratum)*—This ten- to fourteen-foot, slow-moving carpet shark is yellow to grayish brown in color. The young are sprinkled with dark spots. It is found along the Atlantic coasts of North America and Africa and in the Gulf of Mexico. This shark likes to lie motionless in warm, shallow water, sometimes in groups of fifteen or twenty. It has small eyes, smooth skin, and a long tail with almost no lower lobe. Its first dorsal fin is set far back over the pelvic fins and is larger than the second. It has five gill slits, but looks as if it has only four. The fifth is very small and set very close to the fourth. This shark has a small mouth and tiny teeth. The long barbels or feelers on its nose, located just in front of the mouth, are used to find its favorite food: sea urchins, crabs, shrimp, spiny lobsters, and small fish. Its foot-long pups are born alive, twenty to thirty at a time. It seldom attacks unless provoked. *See also* CARPET SHARKS.

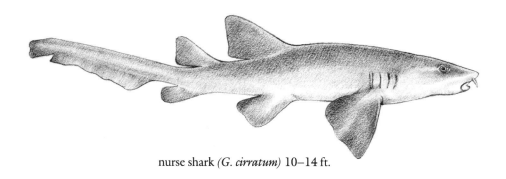

nurse shark *(G. cirratum)* 10–14 ft.

NURSE SHARKS—See CARPET SHARKS.

OCEANIC WHITETIP SHARK *(Carcharhinus longimanus)*—This is one of the most common sharks that is found in deep, warm, tropical waters throughout the world. It almost never goes into shallow water. This requiem shark has a rounded snout; small eyes; very long, paddlelike pectoral fins; a broadly rounded first dorsal fin; and a small second dorsal fin. The twelve-foot body is rounder than those of other sharks, and is light gray to yellow-brown on top, streaked with irregular markings and dirty white underneath. The fins are tipped with white. The upper teeth are triangular and serrated, the lower are spikelike with broad bases. It eats squid, tuna, barracuda, and marlins. This shark often hunts in packs and is not afraid of humans. It is considered dangerous. The thirty-inch pups are born alive in litters of five to fifteen. *See also* REQUIEM SHARKS.

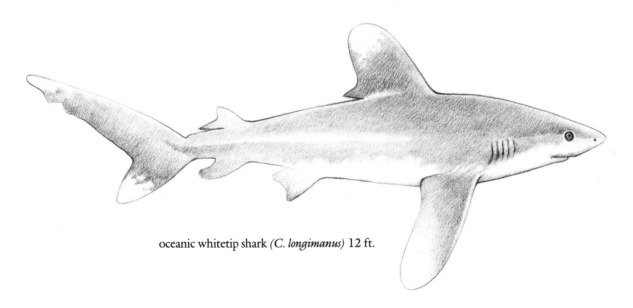

oceanic whitetip shark *(C. longimanus)* 12 ft.

PACIFIC ANGEL SHARK *(Squatinidae californica)*—See ANGEL SHARKS.

PACIFIC PORBEAGLE—See SALMON SHARK.

PACIFIC SHARPNOSE SHARK—*(Rhizoprionodon longurio)* See SHARPNOSE SHARKS.

PACIFIC SLEEPER *(Somniosus pacificus)*—This thirteen-foot spineless dogfish is quite similar to the Greenland shark. This shark is found in the cold deep waters of the north Pacific. It is dark brown to slate gray with rough skin. Its dorsal fins are small and nearly equal in size. It has long, pointed upper teeth with smooth edges; the lower have slanted points. This shark eats halibut, sole, salmon, octopuses, squid, crabs, and seals. Its pups are probably born alive. Other sleeper sharks are known from the Atlantic and Mediterranean. *See also* DOGFISH SHARKS.

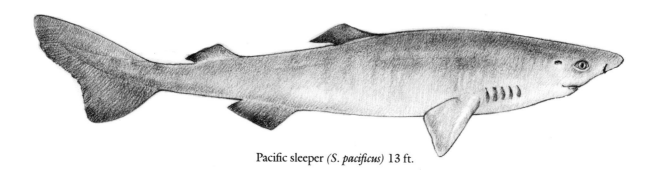

Pacific sleeper *(S. pacificus)* 13 ft.

PEPPERED SHARK *(Galeus piperatus)*—This fourteen-inch catshark is found in warm waters of the Pacific and Atlantic. Its dorsal fins are small and nearly equal in size. The first is set above the pelvic fin. This shark is brown on top and gray underneath. Tiny, black pepper-like spots freckle the stomach. The tail is long and has almost no lower lobe. This shark is a bottom feeder. Its teeth have three to seven points. Its two-inch pups hatch from oval, 1.4-inch, olive green eggs. *See also* CATSHARKS.

peppered shark *(G. piperatus)* 14 in.

PERLON SHARK—See SHARPNOSE SEVENGILL SHARK.

PIGMY SHARK *(Euprotomicrus bispinatus)*—This small dogfish shark is eight to twelve inches long. Its slender body is light brown to dark brown on top with a luminescent underside. A tiny spineless first dorsal fin sits far back on the trunk. This shark is found in warm deep waters of the north and south Pacific, south Indian, and south Atlantic oceans. The upper teeth are needle-sharp. The lower teeth are broader and have a sloping cutting edge. It feeds at the surface and eats squid, small fish, and tiny crustaceans. Its three- to four-inch pups are born alive, eight per litter. *See also* DOGFISH SHARKS.

pigmy shark *(E. bispinatus)* 8–12 in.

PORBEAGLES—See MACKEREL SHARKS.

PORBEAGLE SHARK *(Lamna nasus)*—Also called mackerel shark. This eight-foot mackerel shark is quite similar to the great white, but is smaller and has spikelike teeth. It is found in deep cold water of the South Pacific and Atlantic. It has a pointed snout and a small second dorsal fin. Its torpedo-shaped body is bluish or brownish gray on top and white underneath, with a patch of white on the edge of the first dorsal fin. It is warm-bodied and a fast swimmer. It eats mackerel, cod, squid, and other fish. Its two to four pups are born alive and are twenty-eight inches long. *See also* MACKEREL SHARKS.

porbeagle shark *(L. nasus)* 8 ft.

PORT JACKSON SHARK *(Heterodontus portusjacksoni)*—See BULLHEAD SHARKS.

PORTUGUESE SHARK *(Centroscymnus coelolepis)*—This three- to four-foot long

dogfish shark lives in deep water (about two miles down) on both sides of the north Atlantic. It is dark brown and has short pectoral fins. The small dorsal fins are nearly the same size. They have very small spines. Up to fifteen pups are born alive. They are twelve inches long. *See also* DOGFISH SHARKS.

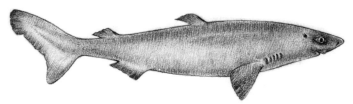

Portuguese shark *(C. coelolepis)* 3–4 ft.

PRICKLY SHARK *(Echinorhinus cookei)*—This very rare dogfish is found in warm

waters of the Pacific Ocean off Baja California. It is quite similar to the bramble shark. Its body is covered with large, pointed skin teeth. The two dorsal fins are nearly equal in size; the first is set far back near the second. This thirteen-foot shark is grayish brown in color with white around the mouth and black-tipped fins. It has molar-like teeth. The pups are about sixteen inches long when born. *See also* DOGFISH SHARKS.

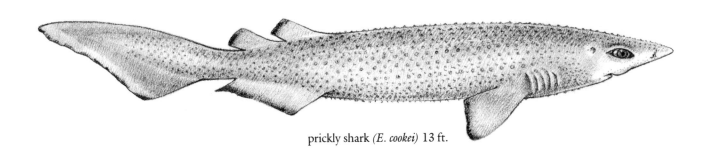

prickly shark *(E. cookei)* 13 ft.

PUFFADDER SHYSHARK (*Haploblepharus edwardsi*)—Also called shy eyes and skaamoong shark. This rare catshark has the peculiar habit of curling its tail over its eyes as if to shield them from the sun when it is taken out of the water. This sluggish-looking shark is about twenty inches long and is a bronze gray with small, dark markings across the back and sides. The belly is white. Its nose is short and round. The second dorsal fin is about the same size as the first. The teeth are small. This bottom dweller lives in cool deep water near South Africa. Its pups probably hatch from eggs. *See also* CATSHARKS.

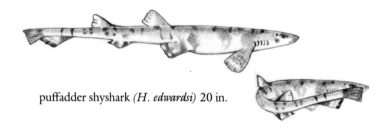

puffadder shyshark (*H. edwardsi*) 20 in.

RAGGED-TOOTH SHARK (*Odontaspis ferox*)—See SAND TIGER SHARK.

REEF SHARK (*Carcharhinus perezii*)—Also called Springer's reef shark and Caribbean reef shark. This seven- to ten-foot requiem shark, resembling the dusky, is found in the Caribbean Sea. It lives in coastal waters and coral reefs and sometimes lies motionless in caves, like nurse sharks, for long periods. It is olive gray on top and yellowish white underneath. Its teeth are serrated; the uppers are narrow and triangular; the lower are spike-like. The reef shark eats fish and rays. Its pups are born alive at twenty-eight inches long. There are usually six in a litter. These sharks rarely attack humans. *See also* REQUIEM SHARK.

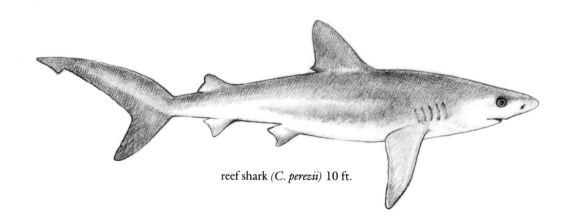

reef shark (*C. perezii*) 10 ft.

REQUIEM SHARKS (Carcharhinidae)—Also called gray sharks, or whaler sharks.

This is one of the largest families of sharks and the ones most often seen by divers. Sixty species are known. All have rounded, flattened snouts, and torpedo-shaped bodies with the first dorsal fin set near mid-back. The lower tail lobe is half as long as the upper. These sharks range in size from three to eighteen feet, most are about seven feet long. Most of them are grayish, but some are olive or brown and some are blue. Their teeth are bladelike, the uppers serrated and broadly triangular. The lowers are narrow and spikelike. These sharks are voracious hunters eating crustaceans, mollusks, smaller sharks, rays, and bony fish. They are common in both warm and cool seas throughout the world. Twenty-two species are found in American waters. The pups are born alive. Although any of these sharks could be dangerous, they usually do not attack unless provoked.

RIBBONTAIL CATSHARKS (Proscyllidae)—This is a family of very small,

deepwater sharks. It consists of two species, but only the Cuban ribbontail catshark *(Eridacnis barbouri)* is found in North American waters. It is found in deep water between Florida and Cuba. This shark has a slender, eleven- to sixteen-inch body with two large dorsal fins of nearly equal size. Its tail has a very long upper lobe and a small lower lobe. This pale gray or tan shark has dark blotches along the back edges of the pectoral and caudal fins and a grayish white belly. It has tiny needle-like teeth. It is not known what it eats. The four-inch pups are born alive, two at a time.

Cuban ribbontail catshark *(E. barbouri)* 16 in.

SALMON SHARK (*Lamna ditropis*)—Also called Pacific porbeagle. This mackerel shark is very similar to the porbeagle, but is only five feet long. It lives in the icy waters of the north Pacific. It is called salmon shark because it feeds on salmon fish. This shark is considered delicious to eat. *See also* PORBEAGLE SHARK and MACKEREL SHARKS.

salmon shark *(L. ditropis)* 5 ft.

SAND SHARKS (Odontaspididae)—Also called sand tigers or ragged-tooth sharks. This is a family of large sharks. There are six species in this family, all very similar. They are found in cool waters throughout the world. They are found in caves and sometimes lie motionless on the bottom. These gray or green-gray sharks have conical snouts and large dorsal fins nearly equal in size with the first placed far back. The spikelike teeth hang out of the mouth, giving them a fierce look. These fish-eaters swallow food whole. They are eight to ten feet long. The best known (because they live well in aquariums) are the ragged-tooth and the sand tiger found in North American waters and the gray nurse shark found in Australian waters. They are not considered very dangerous.

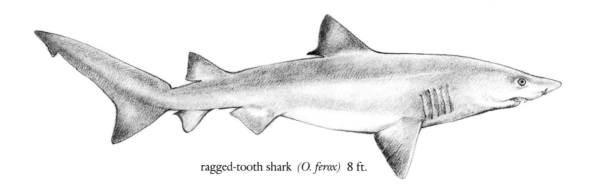

ragged-tooth shark *(O. ferox)* 8 ft.

SAND TIGER SHARK *(Odontaspis taurus)*—This slow-swimming, ten-foot sand

shark is found on the bottom, near the shore in warm and cool waters of the world. It is light greenish gray on top and grayish white underneath, and has yellow eyes. It migrates to deeper water in winter. Its three-foot-long pups are born alive, only two at a time. It looks ferocious because of its large teeth, but is not generally considered dangerous, although it could be. The gray nurse shark of Australia is probably the same species. The ragged-tooth shark *(O. ferox),* common in the Pacific, is smaller and is dark gray with a lighter belly. The bigeye ragged-tooth *(O. kamohari)* found off the coast of Africa is larger and has larger eyes. *See also* SAND SHARKS.

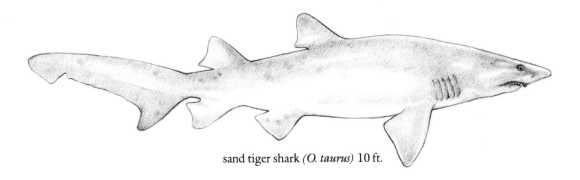

sand tiger shark *(O. taurus)* 10 ft.

SANDBAR SHARK *(Carcharhinus plumbeus)*—Also called brown shark. This six-

to eight-foot requiem shark lives in shallow coastal waters and salty river mouths throughout the world. This shark is migratory and often travels in large groups. It is smaller and stockier than most requiem sharks and has a high first dorsal fin placed more forward. It is brownish gray on top and lighter in color underneath. The upper teeth are triangular and serrated, the lower are spikelike. Sandbar sharks eat small prey—crustaceans, mollusks, and small fish. Pups are born alive, nine to fourteen per litter, and are twenty-four inches long. *See also* REQUIEM SHARKS.

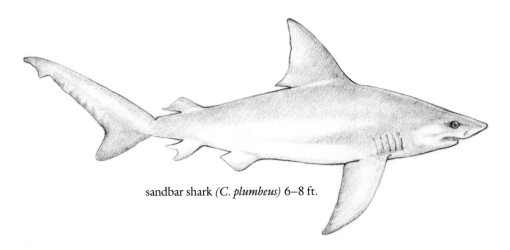

sandbar shark *(C. plumbeus)* 6–8 ft.

SAWSHARKS (Pristiophoridae)—This is a small family of deepwater sharks that resemble the sawfish. Six species are known. They all have long, flat, blade-like snouts with teeth on each side. However, sawsharks have five or six gill slits on the sides of their necks and two long barbels on the underside of their more pointed sawlike snouts. Very small teeth are also found inside the mouth. Their two large dorsal fins are nearly equal in size. Sawsharks are light gray to brownish gray on top and whitish underneath, and can grow to four feet long. Their young are born alive and are twelve inches long. Only one species is found in North American waters. The American sawshark *(Pristiophorus schroederi)* has five pairs of gill slits and very small teeth. It is light gray on top and white underneath and grows to thirty-two inches. It is found off the coast of Florida. *P. warreni* is a sawshark of the Far East and Africa. It has six pairs of gill slits and is four feet long.

American sawshark *(P. schroederi)* 32 in.

SCALLOPED HAMMERHEAD *(Sphyrna lewini)—See* HAMMERHEAD SHARKS.

SCOOPHEAD HAMMERHEAD *(Sphyrna media)—See* HAMMERHEAD SHARKS.

SEVENGILL SHARK *(Notorynchus cepedianus)*—This 8.5 to 10-foot cowshark has seven gill slits on each side of the head. It lives in colder deep waters of the Pacific and Indian oceans and may swim constantly. It is brownish with dark blotches on top and whitish underneath. Its body is long and slender with only one dorsal fin, which is set behind the pelvic fin. The upper teeth are long and pointed, the lower are broad and sawlike. This shark eats smaller sharks and mackerel. Its pups are born alive with up to eighty pups per litter. *See also* COWSHARKS.

sevengill shark *(N. cepedianus)* 8–10 ft.

SHARPNOSE MACKEREL SHARK—Same as shortfin mako. *See* MAKO SHARKS.

SHARPNOSE SEVENGILL SHARK *(Heptranchias perlo)*—Also called perlon. This cow shark is quite similar to the sevengill shark, but is only four feet long and has a narrow, more pointed snout, and lacks the splotches. It lives in deep water all over the world. Its ten-inch pups are born alive, nine to twenty per litter. *See also* COWSHARKS.

sharpnose sevengill shark *(H. perlo)* 4 ft.

SHARPNOSE SHARKS *(Rhizoprionodon)*—The sharks in this group of requiem sharks are all similar. Each has a long pointed snout, long tail, small second dorsal fin set behind the anal fin, and is between 2.5 and 3.5 feet long. The teeth are slightly serrated and narrowly triangular. All three species live in warm, shallow coastal waters and eat small crustaceans and fish. Their pups are born alive, three to five at a time, and are about ten inches long. These sharks differ only in the shape of their teeth, color, and the number of vertebrae. The Pacific sharpnose *(Rhizoprionodon longurio)* is grayish brown. The Caribbean sharpnose *(R. porosus)* is brown or grayish brown, while the Atlantic sharpnose *(R. terraenovae)* is brownish, olive gray, or bluish gray with metallic glints and a few white spots. All have whitish bellies. *See also* REQUIEM SHARKS.

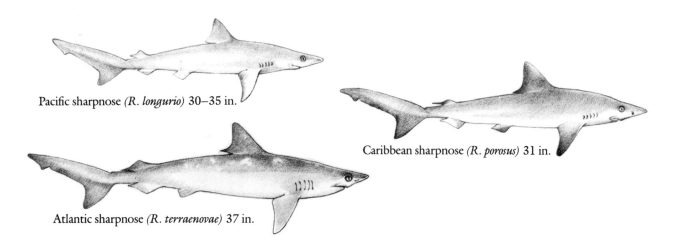

Pacific sharpnose *(R. longurio)* 30–35 in.

Caribbean sharpnose *(R. porosus)* 31 in.

Atlantic sharpnose *(R. terraenovae)* 37 in.

SHORTFIN MAKO(*Isurus oxyrinchus*) —This shark is one of the two species of mako sharks. It is also called bonito, blue pointer, or sharpnose mackerel shark. *See* MAKO SHARKS.

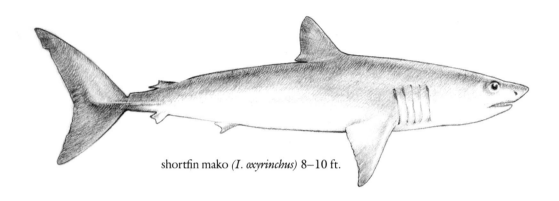

shortfin mako (*I. oxyrinchus*) 8–10 ft.

SHOVELHEAD SHARK—See BONNETHEAD SHARK.

SHY EYES SHARK—See PUFFADDER SHYSHARK.

SICKLEFIN SMOOTHHOUND (*Mustelus lunulatus*)—This smoothhound shark grows to four feet long. It is found close inshore along the Pacific coast from California to Panama. Its slender body is gray or olive brown. Its second dorsal fin is larger than its anal fin and the tip of the lower tail lobe is pointed and often hooked. Its teeth are small and like pavement stones. They are used to crush crustaceans. Pups are thirteen inches long when born. *See also* SMOOTHHOUND SHARKS.

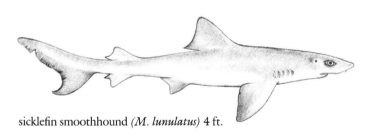

sicklefin smoothhound (*M. lunulatus*) 4 ft.

SILKY SHARK *(Carcharhinus falciformis)*—This ten-foot requiem shark is found in warm waters of the open ocean all over the world. It sometimes strays into coastal waters. This shark is best known for its relatively smooth skin, a result of its small dermal denticles or skin teeth. Its snout is short and rounded. The pectoral fins are long and the loose rear tip of the small second dorsal fin is very long. The silky is brownish or grayish on top and lighter in color underneath. This fast-swimming surface dweller is the most common shark around the Bahamas. It is very curious and sometimes comes near to divers. The upper teeth are broadly triangular with serrated edges; the lower are smooth and narrow with broad bases. It eats squid and small fish. Pups are thirty-one inches at birth and are born in litters of six to fourteen. *See also* REQUIEM SHARKS.

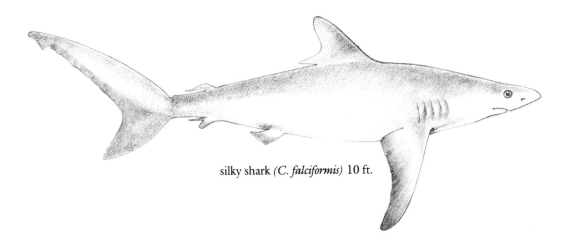

silky shark *(C. falciformis)* 10 ft.

SILVERTIP SHARK *(Carcharhinus albimarginatus)*—Also called inshore white-tip. This common requiem shark is found in reefs near the shores in the Red Sea, Indian Ocean, and western Pacific. This eight-foot shark is gray on top and white underneath, with large, broadly rounded dorsal and pectoral fins edged with white. It is a day feeder and eats fish, rays, and smaller sharks. Its teeth are bladelike. This shark has not been known to attack humans, but it could be dangerous because it is not afraid of humans and there are so many of them near the shore. Its pups are born alive. *See also* REQUIEM SHARKS.

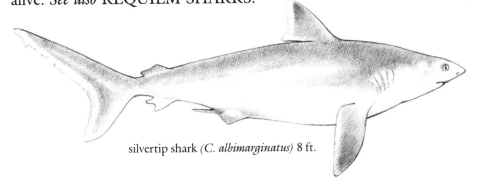

silvertip shark *(C. albimarginatus)* 8 ft.

SIXGILL SHARK *(Hexanchus griseus)*—Also called cowshark and mud shark. This large fifteen-foot cowshark has a long, slim body. It is found all over the world in both warm and cool deep waters. It has six pairs of gill slits and only one dorsal fin set above the anal fin. Its snout is broad and rounded, and its upper tail lobe is long. This shark is dark gray or brown with a whitish belly. It has broad, sawlike teeth on each side of its lower jaw. The upper teeth are sharply pointed. This night feeder occasionally comes to the surface. It eats crustaceans and many kinds of food fish. Its pups are born alive in litters up to a hundred at a time and are twenty-six inches long. *See also* COWSHARKS.

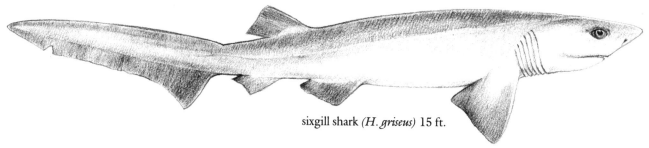

sixgill shark *(H. griseus)* 15 ft.

SKAAMOONG SHARK—See PUFFADDER SHYSHARK.

SLEEPER SHARK—See GREENLAND SHARK.

SMALLEYE HAMMERHEAD *(Sphyrna tudes)*—See HAMMERHEAD SHARKS.

SMALLTAIL SHARK *(Carcharhinus porosus)* —This small requiem shark is only three feet long. Its upper tail fin is one fourth the length of its slender body. The snout is long and somewhat pointed. The second dorsal fin is small and set above the anal fin. Its back is bluish gray, its belly is lighter. This shark lives in warm, shallow coastal waters along the eastern and western coasts of North America and Mexico. The teeth are serrated, the uppers broadly triangular and the lowers narrowly triangular with finer serrations. This shark eats fish, crabs, and other invertebrates. The nine-inch pups are born alive in litters of sixteen. *See also* REQUIEM SHARKS.

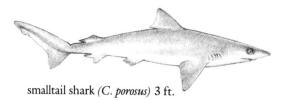

smalltail shark *(C. porosus)* 3 ft.

SMALLTOOTH THRESHER *(Alopias pelagicus)*—One of the three species of thresher sharks. *See* THRESHER SHARKS.

SMOOTH DOGFISH *(Mustelus canis)*—This is one of the most abundant sharks along the eastern coast of North America. It is also one of the best known. It lives near the shore and migrates in large schools—north in summer and south in winter. This four- to five-foot smoothhound shark has a very slender body. The second dorsal fin is larger than the anal fin, and the lower tail lobe is rounded. It is pearl gray to brownish on top with a yellowish or grayish white belly. It can change color to blend in with the background. Its teeth are small and like paving stones. It feeds at night, usually eating crabs, lobster, and shrimp, and it will eat whatever it can find. Its pups are fourteen inches long and are born alive in litters of ten to twenty. *See also* SMOOTHHOUND SHARKS.

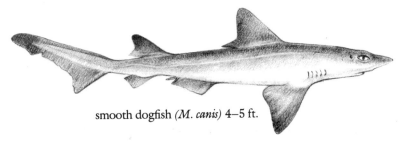

smooth dogfish *(M. canis)* 4–5 ft.

SMOOTH HAMMERHEAD *(Sphyrna zygaena)*—*See* HAMMERHEAD SHARKS.

SMOOTHHOUND SHARKS (Triakidae)—Also called smooth dogfish. This is a family of small to medium-sized sharks (six feet or less.) Thirty-six species are known. They all have slender bodies and large oval eyes. Their skin feels smoother than most sharks because they have small dermal denticles. They have large, spineless dorsal fins. The second is about three fourths the size of the first and is set ahead of the anal fin. The tail fins are short and broad. Most have pavement-like teeth and eat mostly crustaceans. The young are born alive. These sharks are very common and inhabit shallow to moderately deep waters of all oceans. Because there are so many of them, these sharks are popular for laboratory studies. The Florida dogfish, leopard shark, smooth dogfish, and soupfin, as well as all the smoothhounds, belong to this family.

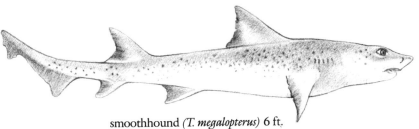

smoothhound *(T. megalopterus)* 6 ft.

SOUPFIN SHARK

SOUPFIN SHARK (*Galeorhinus zyopterus*)—This six-foot shark of the smooth-hound family has a small second dorsal fin set above the anal fin and a very wide lower tail fin. This slim shark lives in warm and cool waters along the Pacific coast of North and South America. It swims in schools in moderately deep water and migrates north in summer and south in winter. It is dark bluish gray on top and lighter in color underneath. Its small teeth are pointed and sharply slanting. It eats many kinds of fish including mackerel, salmon, anchovies, and sardines. It, in turn, is often eaten by humans. The fourteen-inch pups are born alive, thirty-five pups in an average litter. The tope of England and the Australian school shark are very similar to the soupfin. *See also* SMOOTHHOUND SHARKS.

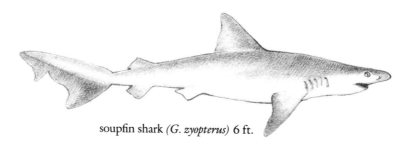

soupfin shark *(G. zyopterus)* 6 ft.

SPINNER SHARK (*Carcharhinus brevipinna*)—Also called large blacktip. This eight-foot requiem shark is found in most tropical waters around the world. It is gray or bronze on top and white underneath. It closely resembles the blacktip, having black tips on the second dorsal, anal, pectorals, and the lower lobe of the tail fin. It has smaller eyes than the blacktip. The first dorsal fin is placed in mid-back and the second is quite small. This fast-swimming shark is often seen in schools near the shore and migrates to offshore in winter. When feeding, it spins up through schools of small fish, often leaping high into the air. It also eats squid, small sharks, and rays. It has sharp, spikelike teeth. The thirty-inch pups are born alive, six to twelve in a litter.*See also* REQUIEM SHARKS.

spinner shark *(C. brevipinna)* 8 ft.

SPINY DOGFISH *(Squalus acanthias)*—This three-foot dogfish has a streamlined body and two dorsal fins, but no anal fin. The second dorsal is smaller than the first. Each dorsal fin is armed with small, poisonous spines which can give nasty wounds, but they are used only in defense. This shark is slate gray or brownish gray with white splotches on top and pale gray or white underneath. It has broad skin teeth with three-pointed spikes. Spiny dogfish live in cool coastal waters of the north Atlantic, north Pacific, the Mediterranean, and Black Sea. In summer it migrates north or goes into cooler deep water. It sometimes swims a thousand miles in a single year. It eats almost anything but prefers small fish, squid, and octopuses. Large packs or schools of thousands have been known to chase schools of fish. Their knifelike teeth point sharply to the back. Based on the rings on their dorsal spines, it is estimated that these sharks live to be at least thirty years old. Their seven pups are born alive and average about ten inches at birth. The mother carries the pups two years before they are born. This is the longest gestation period known for any animal with a backbone. This shark is one of the most hated by fishermen because they ruin fish nets and there are so many of them. However, some fishermen sell them to colleges. Zoology students study the spiny dogfish as the example of a shark. *See also* DOGFISH SHARKS.

spiny dogfish *(S. acanthias)* 3 ft.

SPINY SHARK—See BRAMBLE SHARK.

SPRINGER'S REEF SHARK—See REEF SHARK.

SWELL SHARK *(Cephaloscyllium ventriosum)*—When it is caught, this strange shark can blow itself up like a balloon by gulping water or air. It probably also does this to wedge itself more tightly into its hiding place among the rocky kelp beds where it lives. This 3.5-foot catshark has large oval eyes. Its teeth are small and have three or four points. It is yellowish brown with dark brown saddlelike bars across its back and many round, dark brown spots scattered all over its body. Its first dorsal fin is behind the pelvic fins, and the second is smaller than the anal fin. This bottom dweller is found along the southern Pacific coast of North America near shores in moderately deep water. It hunts at night and eats small fish. The pups are hatched from horny, brown, palm-sized eggs. Long tendrils or threads fasten them to the coral. The pups are six inches long when hatched. Similar species *(C. laticeps* and *C. isabella)* live in Australian and Japanese waters. *See also* CATSHARKS.

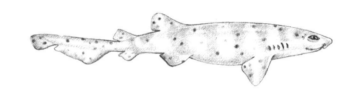

swell shark *(C. ventriosum)* 3.5 ft., before and after ballooning itself

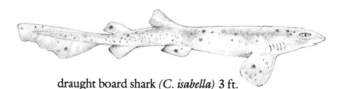

draught board shark *(C. isabella)* 3 ft.

THRESHER SHARKS

(Alopiidae)—This is a family of sharks. Three species are known, all are quite similar. They have enormously long tails. The upper fin of the tail is as long or longer than the body. The tail is used to stun prey. These sharks are found in both warm and cool waters all over the world, mostly in the open sea, but they often wander into cool inshore waters when chasing schools of small fish or squid. They are dark brown or grayish and range in size from ten to twenty feet long. The second dorsal fin is very small. The first is located either over the pelvic fin or just ahead of it. Young are born alive in litters of two to six and are 3.5 to 6.5 feet long—about a third of the adult length! The common thresher shark *(Alopias vulpinus)* has a large first dorsal fin and small, curved spikelike teeth. It is mostly found in deep water, but occasionally swims at the surface. It has four to six pups five feet long. The bigeye thresher *(A. superciliosus)* has an enormous eye and is also a deep sea shark. It is eleven to thirteen feet long and has a warm body temperature. Its pups are thirty-nine inches long. The smalltooth thresher *(A. pelagicus)* has a very long tail, more than twice the length of its body. Its total length is about ten feet.

smalltooth thresher shark *(A. pelagicus)* 10 ft.

TIGER SHARK *(Galeocerdo cuvieri)*—This large (fourteen to eighteen feet) requiem

shark is one of the most dangerous of all sharks. It lives in warm waters both in deep oceans and shallow coastal regions throughout the world, and it sometimes pursues fish into very shallow water. It is the most common shark around Australia and the Caribbean. Its snout is very short and blunt. Its mouth is large with a long groove in the upper lip, and the jaws are powerful. The second dorsal fin is small, and the tail is very long with a pointed tip. Very young tiger sharks are covered with dark spots which change into dark, tigerlike stripes as they grow, but these gradually fade and adult tiger sharks are dark gray or gray brown with yellowish bellies. The teeth are large, razor sharp, and pointed. They have sawlike edges and deep notches on the sides. Tiger sharks are usually sluggish until they smell food, then they are very active. They will eat almost anything; fish, smaller sharks, skates, rays, porpoises, turtles, marine birds, dead whales, or garbage. They often swallow things that cannot be digested. Their pups are born alive and are thirty-two inches long with thirty-five to fifty-five to a litter. *See also* REQUIEM SHARKS.

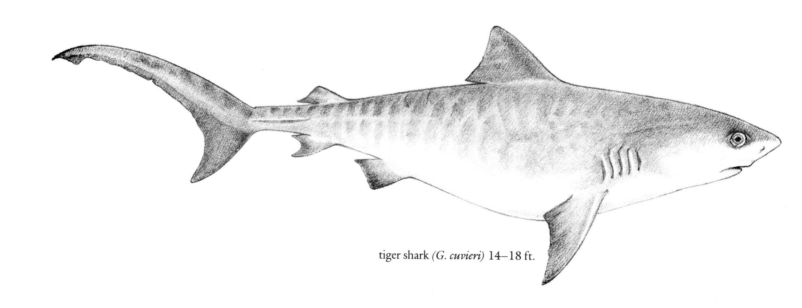

tiger shark *(G. cuvieri)* 14–18 ft.

TOPE *(Galeorhinus galeus)*—See SOUPFIN SHARK.

TSURANAGAKOBITOZAME *(Squaliolus laticaudus)*—This spineless
dogfish is the smallest known shark—only five inches long. Its name is
Japanese for "dwarf shark with long face." It is found in very deep water
off the Philippines and Japan. It is jet black and glows in the dark like a
firefly. Its eyes are large. The upper teeth are needle sharp, the lower have
slanted points. This shark eats squid and small fish. Its pups are born
alive. *See also* DOGFISH SHARKS.

tsuranagakobitozame *(S. laticaudus)* life-size: 5 in.

WHALE SHARK (*Rhiniodon typus*)—This is the largest living fish—up to forty feet long. Some may grow to sixty feet. The tail of a forty-foot whale shark is over ten feet tall from top to bottom. The first dorsal fin is four feet high. This shark is found far at sea in warm oceans all over the world. Its head is broad and flat, like that of a frog, and has an enormous, six-foot mouth at the end of its very short snout. The nostrils have short, blunt barbels. Ridges run along the shark's sides. Its back is reddish brown or greenish gray and is covered with yellow spots and stripes in a checkerboard pattern. Its belly is white. This shark has thousands of tiny, sharp

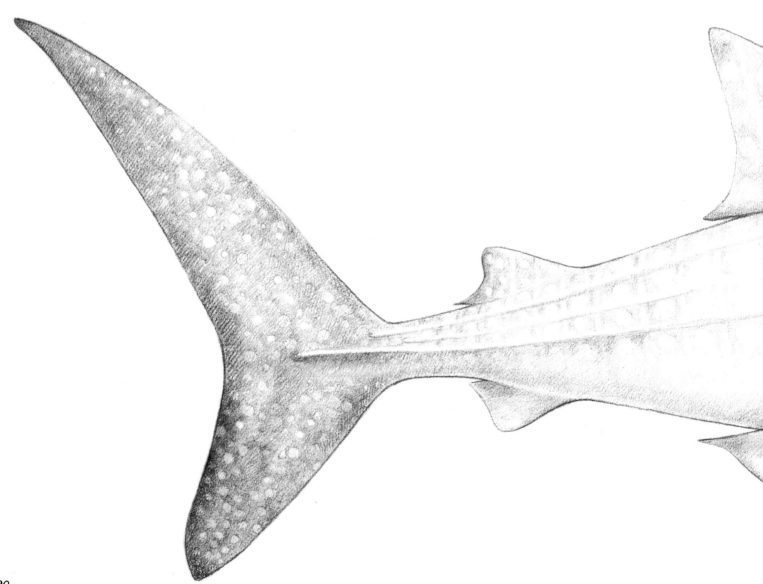

teeth, but eats by straining plankton, squid, and small school fish from the water with sievelike gill rakers. It is a slow swimmer and sometimes eats at the surface with its head up and its tail down. These friendly, curious sharks are dangerous only if they happen to hit a boat or swimmer with their powerful tails or if they are rammed by a boat. The pups hatch from eggs that are twelve by six by four inches. The pups are fourteen inches long when hatched. The whale shark is the only species of the Rhiniodontidae family.

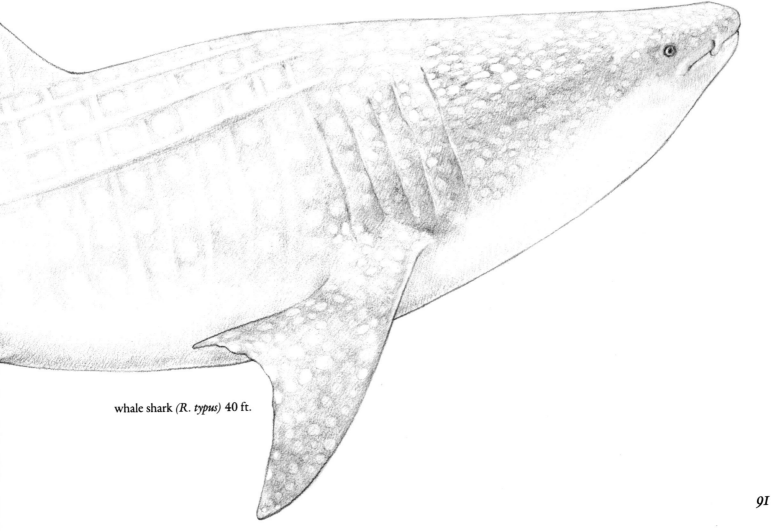

whale shark *(R. typus)* 40 ft.

WHITE SHARK OR WHITE POINTER SHARK—See GREAT WHITE SHARK.

WHITETIP REEF SHARK *(Triaenodon obesus)*—Also called Australian white-
tip. This five-foot smoothhound is found in warm water near the shores
of the Indian Ocean and western Pacific. It has a very short snout
and is brown on top and pale underneath. The tail and dorsal fins are
tipped with white. These sharks will eat almost any fish and are most
active at night. They often gather in lagoons in groups of a hundred or
more. Usually they rest in caves during the day. The pups are born alive.
See also SMOOTHHOUND SHARKS.

whitetip reef shark *(T. obesus)* 5 ft.

WOBBEGONG SHARK *(Orectolobus maculatus)*—This shark is also called car-
pet shark because of its richly colored markings (usually cream on dark
brown) which blend in perfectly with the ocean floor. This six- to ten-
foot shark, the largest of several wobbegongs, rests on the bottom during the day and hunts at night. It has spiky teeth and a fringe of barbels
or feelers around its very wide mouth. It eats crabs, lobsters, and small
fish. The wobbegong lives near the shores of Australia and New Zea-
land. Its pups are born alive. This shark is not dangerous unless stepped
on. Other species live near China and Japan. They differ only in size,
shape, and color of their markings. Because of their beautiful markings,
their hides are sometimes made into leather. *See also* CARPET SHARKS.

wobbegong shark *(O. maculatus)* 6–10 ft.

ZAMBEZI SHARK *(Carcharhinus leucas)*—This is the name given to the bull shark that lives in the Zambezi River. *See* BULL SHARK.

ZEBRA SHARK *(Stegostoma fasciatum)*—Sometimes called leopard shark (different from *Triakis semifasciata*). This ten-foot carpet shark has two fleshy feelers on its snout and ridges on its side like a whale shark. Its body is similar to that of the nurse shark, but it has a very long tail (almost as long as in thresher sharks) with almost no lower lobe. Adults are yellowish white with brown spots. Young are dark brown with white stripes. This shark is found in the western Pacific and Indian oceans. During the day it rests on the bottom. At night it hunts for crabs, barnacles, and shellfish. Its teeth have several points. Pups hatch from oblong egg cases equipped with long threads that hold them to objects on the sea bottom. *See also* CARPET SHARKS.

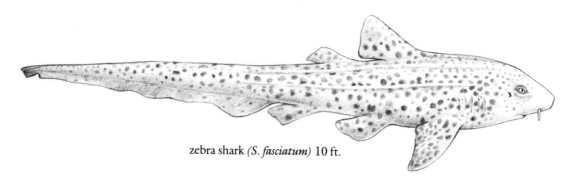

zebra shark *(S. fasciatum)* 10 ft.

Sharks Listed by Family

ANGEL SHARKS (Squatinidae)
 Atlantic angel shark
 Pacific angel shark

BASKING SHARKS (Cetorhinidae)
 basking shark

BULLHEAD OR HORN SHARKS
(Heterodontidae)
 horn shark
 Mexican horn shark
 Port Jackson shark

CARPET OR NURSE SHARKS
(Ginglymostomatidae)
 nurse shark
 wobbegong
 zebra shark

CATSHARKS (Syliorhinidae)
 brown catshark
 chain dogfish
 deepwater catshark
 filetail catshark
 head shark
 longnose catshark
 marbled catshark
 peppered shark
 puffadder shyshark
 swell shark

COWSHARKS (Hexanchidae)
 calf or bigeye sixgill shark
 sevengill shark
 sharpnose sevengill shark
 sixgill shark

DOGFISH SHARKS (Squalidae)
 black dogfish
 Blainville's dogfish
 bramble shark
 cookie-cutter shark
 devil fish shark
 green dogfish
 Greenland shark
 gulper shark
 kitefin shark
 lantern shark
 Pacific sleeper

pigmy shark
Portuguese shark
prickly shark
spiny dogfish
tsuranagakobitozame

FALSE CATSHARKS
(Pseudotriakidae)
 false catshark

FRILLED SHARKS
(Chlamydoselachidae)
 frilled shark

GOBLIN SHARKS
(Scapanorhynchidae)
 Goblin shark

HAMMERHEAD SHARKS
(Sphyrnidae)
 bonnethead shark
 great hammerhead
 scalloped hammerhead
 scoophead hammerhead
 smalleye hammerhead
 smooth or common hammerhead

MACKEREL SHARKS (Lamnidae)
 great white shark
 longfin mako
 porbeagle shark
 salmon shark
 shortfin mako (bonito)

MEGAMOUTH (Megachasmidae)
 Megamouth

REQUIEM SHARKS OR GRAY
SHARKS (Carcharhinidae)
 Atlantic sharpnose shark
 bignose shark
 blacknose shark
 blacktip shark
 blacktipped reef shark
 blue shark
 bull shark
 Caribbean reef shark
 Caribbean sharpnose
 cocktail shark

dusky shark
finetooth shark
Galápagos shark
Ganges River shark
gray reef shark
lemon shark
narrowtooth shark
night shark
oceanic whitetip shark
Pacific sharpnose shark
reef shark
sandbar shark
sharpnose shark
silky shark
silvertip shark
smalltail shark
spinner shark
tiger shark

RIBBONTAIL CATSHARKS
(Proscyllidae)
 Cuban ribbontail catshark

SAND SHARKS (Odontaspididae)
 bigeye ragged-tooth shark
 gray nurse shark
 ragged-tooth shark
 sand tiger shark

SAWSHARKS (Pristiophoridae)
 American sawshark

SMOOTHHOUND SHARKS
(Triakidae)
 brown smoothhound shark
 Florida dogfish shark
 gray smoothhound shark
 leopard shark
 sicklefin smoothhound
 smooth dogfish
 soupfin shark
 whitetip reef shark

THRESHER SHARKS (Alopiidae)
 bigeye thresher
 common thresher
 smalltooth thresher

WHALE SHARKS (Rhiniodontidae)
 whale shark

For Further Reading

Baldridge, H. David. "Sharks Don't Swim. They Fly." *Oceans,* March–April 1982, pp. 24–26.

————· *Shark Attack.* New York: Berkley Publishing Group, 1974.

Blumberg, Rhoda. *Sharks.* New York: Camelot, 1976.

Budker, Paul. *The Life of Sharks.* New York: Columbia University Press, 1971.

Bunting, Eve. *Sea World Book of Sharks.* San Diego: Harcourt Brace Jovanovich, Inc., 1979.

Burgess, Robert F. *The Sharks.* Garden City, New York: Doubleday Publishing Company, 1971.

————· "Sharks vs. Porpoise." *Science Digest,* June 1971, pp. 36–40.

Castro, Jose I. *The Sharks of North American Waters.* College Station, Texas: Texas A & M University Press, 1983.

Clark, Eugenie. "Sharks/Magnificent and Misunderstood." *National Geographic Magazine,* August 1981, pp. 138–186.

————· "Into the Lairs of 'Sleeping' Sharks." *National Geographic Magazine,* April 1975, pp. 570–580.

————· *The Lady and the Sharks.* New York: Harper & Row, Publishers Inc., 1969.

Cousteau, Jacques Y. and Phillippe Cousteau. *Shark: Splendid Savage of the Sea.* New York: Doubleday Publishing Company, 1970.

Cropp, Ben. "When Ocean Giants Meet." *Oceans,* May 1979, pp. 43–46.

Ellis, Richard. *The Book of Sharks.* New York: Grosset & Dunlap, Inc., 1976.

Gilbert, Perry W. "The Behavior of Sharks." *Scientific American,* July 1962, pp. 66–68.

Gruber, Samuel H. "The Bigeye Thresher Shark." *Sea Frontiers,* September/October 1980, pp. 307–308.

Hess, Walter N. "Long Journey of the Dogfish." *Natural History Magazine,* November 1964, pp. 32–35.

Hodgson, Edward S. "An Invasion of Sharks." *Natural History Magazine,* December 1971, pp. 93–102.

Isaacs, John D. and Richard A. Schwartzlose. "Active Animals of the Deep-sea Floor." *Scientific American,* October 1975, pp. 85–91.

Kalmijn, Adrianus, and Kenneth J. Rose. "The Shark's Sixth Sense." *Natural History Magazine,* March 1978, pp. 76–81.

Kenney, Nathanial T. "Sharks: Wolves of the Sea." *National Geographic Magazine,* February 1968, pp. 222–257.

McGovern, Ann. *Sharks.* New York: Four Winds Press, 1976.

McGowen, Tom. *Album of Sharks.* Chicago: Rand McNally & Company, 1977.

Nelson, Donald R. "The Silent Savages." *Oceans,* April 1969, pp. 9–22.

Nolan, Ron S. and Leighton Taylor. "Mini, the Friendly Whale Shark." *Sea Frontiers,* May–June 1979, pp. 169–176.

Soucie, Gary. "In Defense of Sharks." *Reader's Digest,* October 1976, pp. 195–200.

Taylor, Ron and Valerie. "Great White Shark—Predator Which Doesn't Eat People." *Oceans,* May 1979, pp. 38–42.

Zim, Herbert S. *Sharks.* New York: William Morrow & Company, Inc., 1966.

Index